Chris Leonard has written f...
mainly biographies and devo...
of *Leaning Towards Easter* an...
SPCK, and this is her eighteenth published book. She regularly contributes Bible-reading notes to *Day by Day with God* and *Inspiring Women Every Day*, and also enjoys leading creative-writing courses and holidays. Her writing and teaching spring from lifelong faith, love of drawing out all the good things that are in people, and a degree in English and theology. She is married with two grown-up children and lives in Surrey. Her website is at <www.chris-leonard-writing.co.uk>.

This book is dedicated to my mum – who, during the writing, has been bravely holding on to life – and to the people I've met, in writing workshops and elsewhere, who responded so honestly to my pleas for stories about their struggles to hold on . . . and to let go.

HOLDING ON AND LETTING GO

Reflections, Stories, Prayers

———◆———

Chris Leonard

First published in Great Britain in 2009

Society for Promoting Christian Knowledge
36 Causton Street
London SW1P 4ST

British Library Cataloguing-in-Publication Data
A catalogue record for this book is available from the British Library

ISBN 978–0–281–06059–7

1 3 5 7 9 10 8 6 4 2

Typeset by Graphicraft Ltd, Hong Kong
Printed in Great Britain by CPI Bookmarque Ltd, Croydon, Surrey

Produced on paper from sustainable forests

Contents

Acknowledgements

I would like to thank the following people for permission to include pieces of their own writing and for all the checking of the words which they and others did so patiently. Contributors' names are listed in order of appearance. *Denotes second piece by someone listed earlier.

Letting go of the bad, holding on to the good

Julie Warren, Alex Mowbray, Ian McFarlane, Penny Clarke, Jenny Danter, Janet Cornish, Pam Mackenzie, Dorothy Stewart, Liz Ray, Valerie Hunter, Bea Fishback, Alicia Arron, Josephine, Marian Foss, Freda Evans, Alexine Crawford, Steve Elmes, Margaret MacKenzie, Sharman Jeffries, Andy Parr.

Holding on or letting go – in life

Julia Jarrett, Nikki Slater, Ronald Clements, Carol Purves, Christine Barrett, Roger Madge, Ruth Bridger, Anne Ripley.

Letting people go

Edwina Vardey, Rachael Underwood, Coral Kay, Deborah Jacob, Fiona James, Julia Nelson, Sue Wall, Sylvena Farrant, Sylvia Herbert, Mel Commandeur, Eric Leat.

Acknowledgements

Essentials

Morag Bramwell, Ruth Cunningham, Kathleen Gillum, Anne Beer, Tony Stayne, Eric Leat*, Emily Bailey, Gerard Le Feuvre, Louise Terry, Sylvena Farrant*, Alex Mowbray*.

Other stories have been written up by the author.

Introduction

Sometimes it is right to hold on to something, sometimes better to let go. But there is often a creative tension around assessing how to act. And in God's economy, it may be that letting go of old ties makes it possible for God to bless us in new ways. True contemporary stories as well as Bible passages in this book will help us explore different aspects of holding on and letting go in a very down-to-earth way.

'Letting go' is in itself a huge subject. Jesus helps us to let go of negatives like fear, bitterness and greed, while taking hold of his positives such as love, forgiveness and giving. He invites us to share in his ministry of letting 'prisoners' go from poverty, oppression, guilt . . . We explore such things in the first section of this book. The second section deals with the good things we have to let go sometimes, such as security, work, health, even life itself. The third section concerns our letting go of people – maybe through bereavement, or of our children, gradually, as they grow. The concluding section covers 'essentials'. And though my thoughts started with 'letting go', 'holding on' appears throughout the book too – read the rest of this introduction to see how, and why!

Few of us find letting go easy – most want to snatch the role, thing, person or emotion back again. It can feel as scary as abseiling – letting yourself down over the lip of a cliff to dangle on a rope. To let the rope out little by little as you descend towards solid ground involves minute-by-minute trust – of the rope and the people helping. As trust builds, so does relationship and confidence – just as when we let go in life, supported by what seems a perilously thin 'rope' of faith, hope and love. We think we're holding on to it, then find that God is holding on to his, far stronger, rope-cradle of faith, hope and love for – and in – us.

The Old Testament tells many stories of how, despite all the bad things his children throw at him, God finds it hard to let go of us. 'How can I give you up, O Israel?' he agonized. When God does let go he holds on too, just as we hold on to our grown children who reject and hurt us, and hurt themselves. We let them go and can't force them to keep on the straight and narrow, but we pray for them, try to keep in touch and show that we love them, even if we hate the things they're doing.

Letting go and holding on at the same time seems the hardest thing – yet you can't have one without the other. They work together in a creative tension. The sheer difficulty means we cry out for help and so receive God's strength. Letting go of materialism makes our hands ready to hold far better gifts. Letting go of self-reliance and letting God hold on to us, we discover our true selves. Letting go of bitterness and anger involves embracing forgiveness, by minute, by hour, by day, by year – and finding love, forgiveness, maybe even redemption of the original wrong.

We need God's wisdom too. For example, loyalty is a virtue but is this the time to hold on to it? Trying to follow a set of rules over such things is impossible! So much depends on timing – and we don't know the future, only God is outside time. The biggest lesson I've learnt in writing this book is how dependent we need to be on him. Our living relationship with him acts as a torch to show the way, as well as a supporting rope-cradle.

Introduction

Jesus said a seed has to die (let go its hold on life) in order to live – and the same is true for us. Such paradoxes lie at the heart of the gospel – and at the heart of holding on and letting go. That sounds very abstract and philosophical – which is why I'm using stories from people alive today. A few, where stated, are fiction; the rest happened as written, though names have been changed in some cases. The tellers come from different walks of life. Most, but not all, are Christians, of the 'ordinary' rather than the famous or 'professional' kind. I thank every one of them for letting me use their stories to 'earth' and illuminate Bible passages on different aspects of holding on and letting go. Each aspect is a bite-sized piece. Rather than rush through the book, you could read one a day, spending time praying, meditating, reading more around the subject – above all letting the Lord impress on you his love and what he wants to say to you, at this time, about holding on and letting go.

Letting go of the bad, holding on to the good

Letting go of self-sufficiency: holding on to trust in God

The LORD longs to be gracious to you; he rises to show you compassion. For the LORD is a God of justice. Blessed are all who wait for him! O people of Zion, who live in Jerusalem, you will weep no more. How gracious he will be when you cry for help! As soon as he hears, he will answer you. Although the Lord gives you the bread of adversity and the water of affliction, your teachers will be hidden no more; with your own eyes you will see them. Whether you turn to the right or to the left, your ears will hear a voice behind you, saying, 'This is the way; walk in it.'   (Isaiah 30.18–21)

'I'll do it my way, be self-sufficient, living in my own space, not depending on anyone else, nor getting in their way – and if I hit trouble, I won't be weak, I'll get myself out of it.' That's moral strength and integrity, twenty-first-century-style, at least in developed nations. But it isn't God's way – the way of trust and love and community.

What do we most need to let go? I wonder if it's our self-sufficiency and our independence, which inevitably veer us 'to the right or to the left'. How does God feel when we're too independent to hear from him? He might say:

What can I give them? Their wonderful house contains every luxury, every machine to make life easier. Their cars

1

and boat, clothes and accessories all cry 'expensive!' Their business is flourishing and their children, who had the best education money could buy, are busy helping to expand it further.

I would give them friends – but how, when the family closes ranks and keeps itself to itself? I could arrange help in practical ways, but they don't operate like that – they hire any help they need.

I try to give them love – but they won't receive it.

I have given them time, plenty of time, though they don't know it.

Nor do they understand, to misquote John Donne, that 'No family is an island, entire of itself'. They appear utterly self-sufficient, yet they could have been such a joy and strength – a channel of good towards others. But I know that the climate is changing and the seas are rising. The time for independent islands is running out. I weep with compassion for them. But, even with all the power in the universe at my disposal, what can I do?

One-time farmer Julie Warren was never rich and independent like that, but she did find herself forced to let go of everything she loved and relied on – all at once. Only God was left! She writes:

There are times when God expects far too much of me! Of course I do tell him this but I have a feeling he just smiles a little and says, 'Trust me! Let's have another adventure together.'

One of these times arose eventually as a result of the death of my husband at the end of August 1992. In one fell swoop I lost the man I loved, the farm, my home, career and all the animals which had come to mean so much to me over the years. The pain of loss was unimaginable. I was left with huge debts, many of which were not mine. With nowhere to live,

2

what was I to do? And how was God going to bring good out of the situation?

I went to stay with my parents, who were then in their mid-eighties and living only five miles away. I realized that they needed care and took on that role for the next four years until both had died. Then, still living in what had been their bungalow, I worked for six years managing the Christian bookshop in Stratford upon Avon.

Retiring from there I was approached to have some voluntary input at a Christian prayer centre – I'd never even dreamed of that. The director had recognized something which had been in me ever since I was a child – people, including complete strangers, have always come to me for help. At my convent school, Reverend Mother used to find me often in a corridor, comforting some older girl who was in tears. She'd usher us into her office, give us cups of tea and leave me and God to sort out the girl's problems. So, volunteering from time to time at this prayer centre I felt fulfilled again, had a home of my own and things were looking up. Until God said, 'It really is time to sell the bungalow.'

I've always had a passionate longing to experience all that God has for me, to its fullest measure but now I said, 'Well, that's fine for you, Lord, but where am I going to live? I've lost so much in my life already – it's the only thing that's left.'

'Trust me – it's time to sell.'

Me and God have these conversations often. I knew the truth of it. I couldn't pay the mortgage or bills – and so many repairs needed doing. I was using credit cards just to eat! If I sold up I could clear all the debts – no more money worries but nowhere to live either; there wouldn't be anything left over for that.

I went ahead with the valuation in November, determining to put the bungalow on the market after Christmas. At a supper party during the festive season a friend said that her daughter was looking to move into the village.

'She can have my place,' I replied, leaving her my keys so she could have a look round, as I was about to go away.

Eventually the day came, as I knew it would, when all was packed and the house sold to my friend's daughter. Then I left my home of nearly eight years and, with nowhere to go, spent six months wandering from friend to friend. During this time negotiations started with the prayer centre and today I'm on their residential team. My meals are cooked for me to the highest standard and my beautiful bedroom overlooks fields full of sheep and cows, bringing back happy memories of my long-ago life. I'm still dependent on God. I'm past retirement age and my contract lasts only for a year at a time – beyond that my home and future are uncertain. Meanwhile I've had to adapt to living in community 24/7. It's a joy in many ways, very difficult in others, and we all work incredibly hard. Believe me, none of us could do it in our own strength – and holding on to trust in God is still an everyday adventure.

Lord, you're generous, full of mercy and compassion. You long to give us so much, even part of yourself – your Son gave his life for us. But often we're too independent to receive from you – or from others. Help us to let go of our own independence and self-sufficiency so that our hands, our arms, our whole beings have room to hold on to all the wonders you long to give us. And when we try to assert our independence again, help us to laugh at our own silliness and go back to walking in the challenging way you've designed especially for us.

Letting go of self-centredness to discover yourself

He must have been wearing X-ray spectacles that day. As I stood in his presence I knew he had fixed his gaze on my nakedness. It wasn't just me, of course; the whole world was there and yet I felt individual and slightly alone. My palms were sweating, not only from fear of the unexpected but from tightly clutching my life story – for that was all I could take with me. The indescribably dazzling light of his face meant that I couldn't look up and stand up at the same time. My senses were on overload. I never imagined divine silence could carry such a deafening roar.

I looked nervously around the sea of faces and lost count of the vast range of expressions, yet all were full of awe. I didn't know where I was; there were no landmarks – in fact there was no land. Just like the sense of time, I felt my body was suspended, yet I stood on solid ground. How could this be – a place that defied description by its very contradictions? Was it actually a place? More like a state, I thought, and my questions queued up in a desperate search for meaning.

Then I knew – everyone knew – for we were standing before our all-knowing, all-seeing and all-powerful Creator. In his presence the beginning and the end of history seemed compacted into a single moment, like a life-size world atlas folded down to one square millimetre.

Incapable of talking, I had to do something – so raised my arms to offer him the story of my life. Other hands went up. Checking my own, I could see only empty fingers. My mind rushed. Where's my story? Who's got my life? I scanned the crowd in vain, rapidly realizing that we had all lost our lives. Before we could panic, the roar of his silence ceased and everyone stood absolutely motionless.

'Your life is with me now, for I have taken it,' spoke the most terrifying, most comforting voice I had ever heard. The depth of reassurance was so powerful that immediately I felt a sense of belonging, like a reunion after many years with old friends, where words are unnecessary. Strangely, despite so many languages, each person heard and understood the voice clearly. Then my arm shook gently, causing me to look down, expecting my neighbour's nudge – but no. I looked back, then it happened again. I looked down more quickly this time but still saw nothing. As I began to question the logic, a sweet voice came close to me:

'John, can you hear me?'

This time I felt sustained pressure and then a more distant voice . . .

'He's coming round now; stay with him.'

'John darling, it's me, Anna – can you hear me?'

I could hear yet couldn't reply as I was genuinely stranded between realities, like a small boat at the mercy of a strong wind and huge waves. The voice came again – a little louder.

'You're going to be all right; can you grip my finger?'

I did, but was it real? As real as the end of time?

My eyelids flickered; my senses picked up speed enough to appreciate my wife's relieved and smiling face.

She spoke again, mingling warmth and excitement: 'The operation's been successful. The surgeon told me it was touch and go and I said the whole church had been praying. Just think, darling . . . you nearly got to heaven before me!'

That true story of a near-death experience happened to friends of Alex Mowbray, who wrote it down for this book.

Our 'story', I suppose, is the essential 'us' – all that's happened in our lives, who we are, our thoughts and dreams, what we've achieved, the people we love. Does God really want us to let go of all of that? Well, yes . . . and no.

Jesus said:

Anyone who loves his father or mother more than me is not worthy of me; anyone who loves his son or daughter more than me is not worthy of me; and anyone who does not take his cross and follow me is not worthy of me. Whoever finds his life will lose it, and whoever loses his life for my sake will find it.   (Matthew 10.37–39)

2 Timothy 1.12–14 says:

[The gospel] is why I am suffering as I am. Yet I am not ashamed, because I know whom I have believed, and am convinced that he is able to guard what I have entrusted to him for that day. What you heard from me, keep as the pattern of sound teaching, with faith and love in Christ Jesus. Guard the good deposit that was entrusted to you – guard it with the help of the Holy Spirit who lives in us.

Read those two passages again, noting what we're to let go, what we're to hold on to and what he holds on to for us! I find them slightly confusing, raising more questions than answers – so the central questions in Alex's friends' tale become helpful.

'Where's my story? Who's got my life?' One of the key things any novelist or scriptwriter has to decide before starting work is, 'Whose story is this?' If they make Person A the central character, the story will have a different theme, tone and most probably ending, than if the central character is Person B. The whole thing comes back to, 'Through whose eyes are we looking?'

A child will soon learn that her desires are not the only thing in the universe. Christians, growing up, learn the same thing – Jesus, not ourselves, is the central character. We, and those we love, are minor ones. It's not that we lose our identity in some universal cosmic soup, as is the aim of certain Eastern religions. Each individual is important to him. We may find it hard to believe, but he loves us, just as he loves every character that is, was or will be. He'll guard us with his life (literally) but if we try to hang on to life for ourselves, fighting to upgrade our place in the story like a film extra trying to steal the Oscar-winner's lines, then we'll risk losing the abundant life which he's given us. That life is his own – made of humility, love, self-sacrifice . . .

I asked what Alex's friend John felt like, hearing the voice of eternal power, being enveloped in that immense sense of belonging and love, and then coming back to his 'ordinary' life on earth. Alex said John, a curate, didn't want to come back but the voice said it wasn't his time yet, he couldn't stay. Even though he rejoined the wife whom he loved, was he 'homesick'? Or content, knowing God had sent him back with a purpose? John had just two more years on earth in which to serve that purpose – the continuing story of Jesus – with humility, love and self-sacrifice.

Lord, to be self-centred seems to me very 'human' – but it's not how you designed humanity to be. If we each loved you with all our mind and heart and soul and strength, and loved our neighbours as ourselves, this world would be like heaven! So give me a nudge every time I try to make myself the centre of the universe. Help me to let go and realign so that, rather than trying to make you part of my story, I see myself as part of yours. What a privilege that is!

Letting go of power and authority, holding on to servanthood

The Revd Ian McFarlane writes:

Who would have thought that a little piece of plastic could have been so significant? One moment it was there and the next, gone! All I had left was a slip of paper which gave me half an hour to leave by the guardroom gate.

When I joined the RAF as a chaplain I was given my identity card – my 'Twelve-fifty' (1250) – displaying my photo, name, rank and number, height and blood-type. Nothing much to look at, unnervingly it proved the equivalent of Aladdin's 'Open Sesame'. Hefty barriers manned by impassive armed guards opened in an instant; doors into underground bunkers and operations rooms – no problem. Visiting different units at home and abroad – easy – the 1250 made it happen. My identity compressed to credit-card size – with it I had authority and the rights that went with my calling. I could expect responses from all sorts of people and had a place in the scheme of things. Without it I could go nowhere and was a nobody.

Then came the day when I realized that I had to lay down the role of a military chaplain and return to church life in the civilian world. How unprepared I was for the moment of 'clearing' – the RAF's means of ensuring that all bills were paid, all kit returned and nothing left outstanding on your file. The last act was to hand in my 1250. In the administrative centre a young corporal took it without a murmur. He was soon chattering with his colleagues while I, a misty-eyed, shaky, slightly traumatized 45-year-old, felt I had just given up my whole purpose, identity and significance.

For me the experience was temporary, but in that moment I looked into another world – catching an echo of the desolation felt by the voiceless, the powerless, the abused and the marginalized who live their whole lives with little sense of purpose or value.

From where does our power and authority come? Ian's came from his position within the RAF's authority structure, as represented by his '1250'. When he left to become a civilian church minister his authority was of a different kind – no one jumped to it with a 'Yes, Sir!'

Jesus' power and authority remind me more of the civilian Church than the RAF model. He had all authority in heaven but during his earthly ministry spoke and acted within his Father's authority structure, rather than trying to exercise it on his own behalf. He identified with those who never had authority – 'the powerless, the abused and the marginalized'. Ultimately he let go of all the power and authority he could have claimed on the cross (no one took it from him!). But at that point, as a dying servant, his purpose and value in his Father's eyes reached new heights. How interesting that it was military officers who recognized Jesus' authority. They too would have obeyed orders, even when that meant laying down their lives – and knew that their own authority came only through a higher one. 'And when the centurion, who stood there in front of Jesus, heard his cry and saw how he died, he said, "Surely this man was the Son of God!"' (Mark 15.39).

A centurion came to him, asking for help:

> Lord, I do not deserve to have you come under my roof. But just say the word, and my servant will be healed. For I myself am a man under authority, with soldiers under me. I tell this one, 'Go,' and he goes; and that one, 'Come,' and he comes. I say to my servant, 'Do this,' and he does it' . . . Then Jesus said to the centurion, 'Go! It will be done

just as you believed it would.' And his servant was healed at
that very hour.   (Matthew 8.8–9, 13)

I'd been listening to radio reports of riots escalating into a
tribal war, following a disputed election in Kenya, and found
myself wondering how many times disasters follow people's
refusal to let go of power – not only politicians and not only
in Africa. That's how the idea for this book began, yet I
had difficulty in finding volunteers to tell their smaller-scale
stories. I'm sure most of us have struggled with letting go
of power to some degree but clearly it's a difficult subject –
maybe even one of the last taboos!

So here's an account I heard of a growing church which
needed a junior minister to share the load. Once that person
was established, the senior minister took a much-needed
three-month sabbatical. On his return he found the church
in turmoil, with different groups at loggerheads and much
talking behind backs. The junior minister made matters
worse by taking sides.

For months the senior minister tried to re-establish
peace and order; he brought in outsiders to help but the
situation became worse. The junior minister would barely
communicate with him. The senior minister could hardly
sleep. Finally he went on retreat, seeking God alone for
several days. God spoke specifically, through that day's reading in the Northumbria Community's *Celtic Daily Prayer*
(HarperCollins Religious, 2000). Words which Clement of
Rome wrote in the first century AD gave such precise advice
on his exact predicament that he knew he had to let go of
power and control, of thinking that he had to sort it all out.
He understood that, though the situation wasn't his fault,
as leader he had become the blockage and nothing would

11

be resolved until he moved on. His role as servant to that particular church had ended – the work was bigger than he was. He had to lay down his reputation too. In the end the church survived in a smaller form and the senior minister went on to enjoy a fruitful ministry elsewhere.

Lord, letting go of power and control seems so very hard for us – yet true authority and power come only from you and you laid yours down for us. Help us to have the same attitude as Christ Jesus, who 'did not consider equality with God something to be grasped, but made himself nothing, taking the very nature of a servant' (Philippians 2.6–7).

Letting go of material treasures, holding on to eternal ones

Store up for yourselves treasures in heaven, where moth and rust do not destroy, and where thieves do not break in and steal. For where your treasure is, there your heart will be also. (Matthew 6.20–21)

I'm writing this as the world heads into deep recession. The accustomed financial security we've enjoyed seems to have evaporated overnight. With no help from moths, rust or swag-bag thieves, all of our materialism is being shaken. So what is this treasure in heaven? Is it located in secret bank vaults, guarded by goblins, or angels? Do heavenly misers gloat over how vast are their particular piles of gold? Hardly! I believe it's riches of a kind beyond our earthbound imaginings – distilled love, personified ultimately in Jesus. Without love we're 'an empty gong and a clashing cymbal'. Our life's achievements and possessions are worthless, fit only to be let go – burnt up like hay and stubble.

Letting go of the bad, holding on to the good

Of what are you most ashamed? A group of mainly non-Christians were discussing this, in a light-hearted way, referring to their teenage years. I kept quiet at first because, though deeply ashamed of certain things in my youth, I have never once taken illegal drugs, drunk myself paralytic, had an affair, even smoked a cigarette. Finally I admitted to having been a boringly 'good' teenager, except when grumpy or self-conscious. Shyness led to my excluding people. I worried myself sick about things, became mean-spirited – in other words I wasn't the most loving person. We gain entry to heaven through Jesus but the Bible says we build up treasure in heaven through the way we live, here on earth. Rather than outward goodness (keeping the law and avoiding the more sensational sins) I think that has to be about godly, unselfish attitudes like love – love for people as well as for God. Even the worst recession can't rob us of such things!

Penny Clarke wrote this about holding on to love's treasure on earth – and what will live on when the physical evidence of it disappears:

I looked round our house the other day and thought, our poor son, Jonathan. When David and I finally go, there will be so much for him to clear away. We really ought to start having a mighty turnout.

Where to begin? Well, what about all those letters, carefully hoarded over the years? First the one written to my father by his mother on his twenty-first birthday. Being a widow, she used black-edged notepaper – something never seen these days, I imagine. It wished him everything he could want in his life and told of her love for him. Then there were the letters written by my father to my mother from the day they met until his death. Those, too, are full of love.

I have letters written by me to my mother, both from school and when I stayed with my grandparents in the holidays. Always ending with a page of hugs and kisses. Among them is a little notebook with some of my very first poems 'what rhymed'! Then there are letters written to me when my mother died – showing how she was loved and would be missed. There are letters I wrote to my parents-in-law from Singapore when David and I were first married. At my request they kept them as a diary of our stay there.

Then a letter written from David to me in hospital when Jonathan was born. A very special one this. Letters written by Jonathan, and in particular one to the tooth fairy saying sorry but he had swallowed his tooth, and please, could she still come? She did! Letters to Father Christmas, homemade cards for Mother's Day. Letters from boarding school, so homesick at first, but gradually becoming happier. Tears still come to my eyes when I read them again.

The thread through all these is love and memories. They can never be taken away, but I suppose one day I will read these letters once more and know the time has come to let them go. But not yet.

Think I'll tackle the cupboard under the stairs tomorrow!

I find de-cluttering incredibly hard, so Jenny Danter's imagined story both moved and challenged me. It's about an ultimate letting go of everything but love.

'Will you hurry and choose which things you're taking!' The cleaner's voice was commanding, cutting insensitively across the old lady's heart.

Those 'things', as she put it, were the remainder of Pam's quiet, unassuming but precious life. The box in front of her was the last thing remaining in this house which had been a home to her family for almost a century.

Letting go of the bad, holding on to the good

A solitary tear rolled down Pam's soft crinkly face as she looked lovingly at all her treasures collected together in that box. Now here she was, facing the hardest decision, the beginning of the end. Which of her treasures should she take to share the limited space of a care-home room? She felt discarded, put out, pushed from her own home. Her mind struggled to comprehend.

Slowly Pam bent down and with her arthritic hand picked up a fragile posy of dried flowers. She fingered it lovingly and smelt it, laughing. Her eyes closed and she relived the intense joy it brought to her mind. Once again she was the most beautiful lady dressed in white; slim, upright, hair shimmering and her body trembling with excitement. He was waiting for her; each chosen for the other, their lives to be joined as one. More tears fell. Pam sighed and jolted herself out of yesterday. He was dead and gone. 'Always tomorrow,' so everyone had said. Gently she replaced the flowers and carefully lifted the dusty photograph beside them to her face. Could she identify the smiles on the boys' faces?

'Oh please God, don't take my mind. Can a mother abandon her sons? No, no,' she cried, clutching her photo and weeping within.

Shattering the privacy and quiet the voice commanded again, 'That's it. Taxi's here. Made your choice?'

A moment's pause as Pam collected herself, she then stood as upright as she could, her aged hands held close to her heart – and turned to go.

'They can all stay here in our home, where they belong.'

Peaceful and content, she knew her treasure would always be in her heart.

Spend some time thanking God for all your eternal treasures of love and pray for those who, for a while, have to face loss.

Letting go of our 'rights'

Blessed are those who mourn, for they will be comforted.
(Matthew 5.4)

Mourning takes many forms and proceeds through many stages in a gradual process of letting go. Grief overwhelms, obscuring everything else – though in allowing themselves to be comforted, mourners may catch glimpses of life beyond it. But what if a person 'misses' someone of whom they have no memories, who never existed? Can that person be comforted? What if someone has to let go of a 'right' such as the right to vision, hearing, mobility – or the right to marry and bear children? What process might ease their letting go?

Janet Cornish, a funeral arranger from Woking, writes:

Like many girls, through my childhood and teenage years I believed that when I grew up I would marry and have children. I entered my twenties, keen to begin my teaching career before doing what I really wanted – to become a mother. Meanwhile, enjoying the independence of my single status, I took exciting holidays, bought a house, moved up the career ladder . . .

In my thirties fear crept in, then intensified – might I never fulfil this deep desire to have children? I don't believe that having a child is a right, even though many people do. In my forties, though, I had to admit that I would never become a mother – and experienced full-blown grief for the children I'd never bear.

By then I was working in the funeral business and began to understand that the grief I was experiencing followed a similar pattern to that of the clients I met day by day, as they dealt with the actual death of a loved one. Whereas their grief was completely acceptable and understood, my experience remained hidden and certainly not understood by most people.

One of the saddest occasions in my professional life occurred when a family who asked us to deal with the practical business of disposing of the body insisted that there should be no form of service whatsoever. Of course we respected their wishes – but not to mark the passing of a life at all appeared to me to be omitting a vital stage in the grieving process. This started me thinking – should I not be honouring my grief by marking my own 'letting go' in some way?

Deciding this was too important an issue to ignore, but not wanting to be too dramatic and 'over the top', I pondered for a long time. Finally, with the help of trusted friends I explored the idea of putting together a 'letting go' service, despite there being no recognized blueprint for this, no book to tell me what to do. With a blank piece of paper in front of me – literally – I wrote. Feelings of deep sadness, anger, frustration and confusion found an outlet.

As with any funeral service, in mine moments of ordinariness mixed with great poignancy. Friends put no pressure on me to 'move on' and for that I'm very grateful. I did experience a feeling of 'letting go and preparing for what's next'. In some ways that's frustrating because I don't know what's next and am left with the feelings of emptiness and absence that many experience following the busyness surrounding a loved one's funeral. However, I've been encouraged by how this act of 'letting go' has enabled me to tell my story, by how it has encouraged, challenged and enlightened others – and brought out into the open what was such a hidden grief.

After reading this poem which Janet wrote to prepare for her service of 'letting go', you might like to use it as a prayer, either for yourself or for someone you know who has had to let go of their 'rights' – perhaps to a much-loved person or a cherished dream.

Open Hands
I sit with open hands
Heavy with the weight of
Unfulfilled dreams
Empty desires
Bitter disappointments
And misplaced hopes.

Questions punch the air
As I demand answers
From a silent God.
What did I do that was so wrong?
Why punish me in this way?
Why don't you answer me?
Why? Why? Why?

Eventually I realize
These are open hands.
Not clenched and angry
But open and willing to let go of the
Resentment
Bitterness
And bewilderment.

These are open hands
Waiting in eager anticipation
Ready to receive
New dreams
New desires
New hopes
Ready at last to receive
God's generous blessings.

Hold on for the rights of the marginalized

'Do not think that because you are in the king's house you alone of all the Jews will escape. For if you remain silent at this time, relief and deliverance for the Jews will arise from another place, but you and your father's family will perish. And who knows but that you have come to royal position for such a time as this?'

Then Esther sent this reply to Mordecai: 'Go, gather together all the Jews who are in Susa, and fast for me. Do not eat or drink for three days, night or day. I and my maids will fast as you do. When this is done, I will go to the king, even though it is against the law. And if I perish, I perish.'

(Esther 4.13–16)

Esther, one of the Jews whose family was carried into captivity in Babylon, found herself chosen to be one of the king's concubines – not a particularly 'Jewish' thing to do, I would have thought. She found favour with King Xerxes who ruled over a huge tract of the then-known world and saved him from an assassination plot. But during her years in that court she 'kept secret her family background and nationality just as [her uncle] Mordecai had told her to do' (Esther 2.20). I wonder what that felt like? Later, when corrupt men of power plot to have all the Jews killed, Esther may be in a unique position to save her own poor and marginalized people. But she knows that it is a huge risk!

I met my friend Pam Mackenzie when she had returned from teaching abroad and embarked on an MA and then a PhD in education. Esther's story is very special to her. She writes:

I knew that God was calling me to work with marginalized and oppressed people – especially with children, in the field of education. As I visited tribal regions in India and

Bangladesh the ideas started to become a little clearer. Friends suggested that I set up an organization to facilitate them. I was very reluctant. Wouldn't moving in this direction mean that I would have to give up everything? I had little in material terms, but I wanted to hang on to myself – make my own decisions, run my own life, earn my own money, have my own home, friends, church and culture.

In the end God spoke to me unmistakably through the book of Esther. Now I live most of the year in India, working for very little financial gain for the development charity which we set up to promote and facilitate multilingual education for the most marginalized groups in several South Asian countries. Working in those very different cultures hasn't been easy, especially as a single woman. I've lived at breaking point with frustration, sometimes. Yet I realized the other day that the greatest moments of God's history-changers in the Bible usually came when they were in captivity in a foreign land. Moses and Joseph both rescued their own people in Egypt. Young Esther, although queen in a foreign country, gave up her right to her own life for the people of God. Her famous words, 'If I perish, I perish' meant that she did not know the outcome of what she was about to do. For Daniel and his friends and for Nehemiah it was the same. But, because they submitted to the Lord, the grace, or favour, of God was on each one of them. Each found favour with the ruling authorities of a religion and culture alien to them.

Although we cannot claim these things for ourselves, and very often get things wrong, we can claim that we are the people of God; we too can see the amazing hand of God in our lives when we submit ourselves and our plans to his. It isn't easy – like Esther, we don't know how things will turn out. But I have seen God open doors into the highest authorities, who have listened. Sometimes there's opposition and, like Nehemiah, we have to find ways around the difficulties in order to keep on with the work – but I've seen policy and practice change in several nations and among powerful international agencies.

I don't want to give the impression that it's just me doing this. Many, from completely different backgrounds, nationalities, aid organizations and religious affiliations, have been very much involved. I believe that God brings the right people together at the right time to fulfil his purposes.

The UN affirms it is imperative that all children should be in school for their primary years. But what if the quality of the education they receive is poor? Because they spoke a tribal, rather than the official state language, children I work with used to be able to understand nothing that went on in school. Suffering the negative attitudes of teachers who thought them stupid, they underachieved and dropped out. Most, being first-generation learners, could find no help from their parents or communities and if children remained uneducated, those communities remained voiceless and open to exploitation.

These same children now enjoy the experience of school as never before. They're first given the opportunity to learn in their mother tongue, and then to add other languages they need, through a multilingual education programme. They learn fast, gain confidence for mainstream education and for life – and how their whole communities benefit!

I've been privileged to see dramatic changes in the lives of many from remote and marginalized communities. In relation to the vast needs of children from ethno-linguistic minority communities in Asia, Africa and other places, these changes remain small and fragile, but we will continue to work as long as we have the ability to do so and the favour of God and of people in our lives. Eventually, we see how God has worked – and knowing that we have played a part makes all our sacrifices worthwhile.

Spend some time praying for all those, like Pam, who let go of their own rights in order to take on what can at first appear to be an almost impossible fight on behalf of the poor and marginalized who cannot fight for themselves.

You can see more about Pam's work on <www.infd.org.uk>.

Letting go of a wrong self-image, holding on to God's image within yourself

When Eliab, David's oldest brother, heard him speaking with the men, he burned with anger at him and asked, 'Why have you come down here? And with whom did you leave those few sheep in the desert? I know how conceited you are and how wicked your heart is; you came down only to watch the battle.'

'Now what have I done?' said David. 'Can't I even speak?' . . .

David said to Saul, 'Let no-one lose heart on account of this Philistine; your servant will go and fight him.'

Saul replied, 'You are not able . . . you are only a boy, and he has been a fighting man from his youth' . . .

But David said to Saul, 'Your servant has been keeping his father's sheep . . . [and] killed both the lion and the bear; this uncircumcised Philistine will be like one of them, because he has defied the armies of the living God.'

(1 Samuel 17.28–29, 32–34, 36)

Who do you think you are? David knew who he was – the youngest of his father's eight sons – useful for running errands and looking after sheep. He must have been proud to be sent with provisions to his three oldest brothers – fine, brave soldiers on the front line, fighting for King Saul.

Eagerly he asks the first soldiers he finds about the army's response to the enemy's challenge.

It's always interesting how different people see the same thing in very different ways. Eliab's view of his brother, as well as of the army's situation, couldn't have been more different from David's. His little brother was conceited, wicked, shirked his duties, had no understanding of what was going on – here only for entertainment or thrills – the little brat!

David's response to that comprehensive put-down was that he was having none of it. The reason? He, the youngest in the family, the lowest of the low, knew Almighty God was protecting him, and even the sheep, from bears and lions. If he and sheep were worth that much, then weren't these fine soldiers worth even more? David toddles off again to see how King Saul's heroic soldiers are responding to the foolish giant Goliath's challenge. After all, how could Goliath possibly hope to win if he defied the armies of the living God?

Next thing, young David is summoned to speak to King Saul himself. Suitably polite but not overawed, David still can't understand why the army is cowering in stalemate instead of rising to the challenge. His trust in God, rather than in force or armour, is childlike and complete. Perhaps that is what makes him, in the end, a great king, or at least a great citizen of the upside-down kingdom which people can't enter unless they become as little children.

Who we think we are has a direct effect on our attitudes and so on almost everything we do. Too often, negative re-marks stick, right from our childhood years, preventing us from doing so much. Remarks like 'you're stupid, clumsy, hopeless, bad at speaking/writing/maths, a slut or coward, ugly, uncaring, unlovable' – need I go on? The truth is that we are in God and he is in us, transforming us. We can let him release the hold those remarks have over us. If we truly believe that we are children of the most high God then whom should we fear? We wouldn't be proud of ourselves, only of God. We may, of course, remain bad at maths or whatever, but God's family includes others who are good at it, so what's the problem? And even if no one else loves us, he does; he finds us beautiful, puts his hope in us, has important work for us to do – and even greater things for us to be. So let's hold on – not to a wrong self-image but to a right God-image of ourselves – and of those who would challenge this. And then . . . who knows what 'enemy giants' may fall, or what good may happen?

Dorothy Stewart, editor of *A Book of Graces* (SPCK, 2009), writer and writing coach who lives in Suffolk, here tells some of her experience of these things.

We talk at least once a week. Sometimes I ring, sometimes she does and if I miss her call, I always ring back. After all, she's my mum. It's good to stay in touch even if we do live 600 miles apart. But yesterday afternoon, when I picked up her message and called, I hit stormy water again. I'd been out promoting my first children's book. Fewer than thirty pages, it's for little ones, has gorgeous illustrations and I'm pretty thrilled with it.

'Oh, that book,' she sneered. 'Trivial thing.' And then she commented that the big book of prayers I'd done a few years back was far too big, ridiculous.

Her words stung. Pushing sixty yet reduced close to tears, I felt yet again like the little girl who could never get anything right. I remembered all the occasions when I had tried so hard. And failed. But today, suddenly, I know that this situation isn't about me and never was. I was not a wicked but a timid child, scared of doing anything wrong. My children's picture book may be small, but it's not trivial. It carries a message of God's love to little ones. My book of prayers may be large but it's not ridiculous: it's well thought-out for its market. No. This is what a friend calls SEP: someone else's problem.

For so many years, I've been hanging on, twisting myself out of shape to please, trying to win a 'well done, good girl'. Now, at last, I recognize it isn't going to come. It is time to let go and hand it over to God along with the garbage can of pain I've carried round for all these years.

I'll still ring. But it's God's 'well done' I'll care about now.

Some months after Dorothy wrote that piece she emailed me:

My mum died a month ago, in December. In October, suddenly she'd become very ill. I'd rushed up to her bedside where God gave us true reconciliation and new love for one another. Mum even introduced me proudly to people as 'my daughter, the writer'. After she died, when clearing her house I found my books which I had sent to her each time on publication. She'd written her name in the big book of prayers of which she'd spoken so unkindly – each page containing a prayer which I'd written had its corner turned down. She had really worked through it. I realized that her harsh words must have come at a time when she was suffering nicotine deprivation in hospital. There's always a reason . . .

I realized then that the last sentence I'd sent you for the book, Chris, was more my aspiration than strictly true. I still cared very much about having my mother's approval – and even though it came late, that huge blessing washed away years of hurt. And yes, I know, that was God's doing too!

Lord, when – perhaps because of someone else's harsh words – our self-image becomes as distorted as an anorexic's view of herself in a mirror, help us to come back to you to find the truth. Remind us, as St Paul urged young Timothy, 'Fan into flame the gift of God, which is in you . . . For God did not give us a spirit of timidity, but a spirit of power, of love and of self-discipline' (2 Timothy 1.6–7). Help us to let go of shame, misery, rejection and self-denigration and, holding on instead to the truth through your eyes, learn to walk in freedom, courage and joy. Amen.

Letting go of the wrong kind of certainty, holding on to love's truth in humility

While Jesus was having dinner at Matthew's house, many tax collectors and 'sinners' came and ate with him and his disciples. When the Pharisees saw this, they asked his disciples, 'Why does your teacher eat with tax collectors and "sinners"?'

On hearing this, Jesus said, 'It is not the healthy who need a doctor, but the sick . . . I have not come to call the righteous, but sinners' . . .

A man who was demon-possessed and could not talk was brought to Jesus. And when the demon was driven out, the man who had been mute spoke. The crowd was amazed and said, 'Nothing like this has ever been seen in Israel.'

But the Pharisees said, 'It is by the prince of demons that he drives out demons.'   (Matthew 9.10–13, 32–34)

Certainty or, to give it a less polite gloss, dogmatism, can be a terrible thing – one which Jesus fought against throughout his ministry on earth. In the end it killed him – except that it didn't, because he was the man who burst through even that most certain of certainties, death. Today we see Pharisees as the 'baddies' of the Gospels – not like us, of course. Or do some of us, like the Pharisees in Matthew's story, keep away from con men, drunkards, mediums, the promiscuous, basking in the certainty that we're pure and following God's will as laid out in the Bible? Will we find out, in heaven, that guys we've demonized are, in his eyes, truer servants than we've ever been?

When I heard Polly Toynbee say on Radio 4's *Moral Maze* that liberals like herself have had to fight the churches every inch of the way over human rights issues such as race and the place of women, I thought: there's truth in what she's saying. Why do Christians cling to rigid opinions in the name of our faith, even when Jesus' attitude clearly differs?

This certainty, this dogmatism, seems endemic within humankind, a very real enemy. Emily Bailey, whose story appears later in this book, told me she thought the best thing done during a couple of years' development work in a remote area of Zambia was to persuade the Zambians that they weren't inferior to white people. At first their Zambian friends had been quite certain that Jesus was white (which he wasn't!). Because 'God blessed white people', the Zambians couldn't look Emily and her husband in the eye.

'Please, stop calling us Bwana and Madam. You are our brothers and sisters, call us Emily and Richard.' In the end, certainty lost out to love, whereupon Emily and Richard became decidedly unpopular with some white farmers, who had become racists after suffering at the hands of black people when farming in Zimbabwe. Years of white supremacists treating black people as inferior had fuelled that black rebellion and aggression. So many conflicting certainties –

people need to let go. Or, as Emily put it, 'Grace has to break the cycle somewhere.'

Nearer to home, I've been reading a *Radio Times* interview heralding David Attenborough's TV series on Darwin. Did you know that Christians send Attenborough letters rejoicing that he'll burn in hell? Rod Liddle, the interviewer, sympathized with Attenborough – the police had to be called in when some of the subjects of a documentary Liddle made about Christian fundamentalists found out where he lived. The way some Christians defended their 'certainties' had alienated both men, driving wedges between them, Christians and God – how sad!

Equally, scientists know they have to let go of accepted certainties like Newtonian physics, keeping open minds in order to experiment properly, for example in the counter-intuitive world of quantum mechanics. Not a few have had to let go of the secular 'certainty' that no serious scientist believes in God – convinced perhaps by evidence about Jesus or because the Holy Spirit touches them, demonstrating his love and allowing a relationship to develop, real and beyond doubt.

Life coach and media producer/presenter Liz Ray writes of some 'letting go' which happened while she was in India on a course:

> One of my illuminating experiences in India was how less is so definitely more when it comes to sharing spiritual beliefs. I interpreted a few dreams for people (I had delivered a training seminar on 'ancient-Hebraic' dream interpretation as part of my qualification). The rest of the time I tried to listen rather than hold forth on my own beliefs. I've found that God seems to move in direct proportion to my letting go in this way.

One amazing young guy has emailed me since that course, sharing so much about his personal life. He's been praying at bedtime that God would direct him through his dreams and has been dreaming prolifically ever since. His emails are now filled with inspirational quotes on issues such as grace – surprising since, so far as I'm aware, he's not a Christian and doesn't know that I am.

Another girl wept when I interpreted her dream. After ten years she'd finally understood that her dream showed God's specific protection at a very vulnerable time in her life. She has an amazing vision to bring communities together, so I sent her a link to a friend's Christian social action project. An excited email came back telling me that she'd been in touch and was hopeful for what might develop.

When I did share my own spiritual journey with someone I particularly befriended, I included the ups and downs and unfinished ends of my Christian experience. It's the most vulnerable I've been with anyone outside Christian circles – and it created a strong bond of trust. She spoke publicly about how privileged she had felt and, back in the UK, she's becoming a close friend.

I'm coming to believe that our certainties serve to disconnect us, whereas the essence of spirituality – of God's love – is connection. I think I'm finally beginning to get the connection back . . .

Lord, you are the truth – and you're a person, not a dogma. We can be certain of you – but I have the feeling that, if I met you face to face, as the people in the Gospels did, you might make me very uncertain about opinions which I hold fast now. Help me not to alienate people by trying to defend you. How stupid that sounds, me trying to defend the Almighty! Jesus, you worked through love and vulnerability, reaching out without fear or favour. Your certainties were rooted in relationship – that the Father loved you. Hardly had you said a word before some people followed you. Help me to keep quiet sometimes, to prefer showing above telling, to let you do the convincing, Holy Spirit. Keep me humble, keep me connected.

Letting go of perfectionism

As they were walking along the road, a man said to him, 'I will follow you wherever you go.'

Jesus replied, 'Foxes have holes and birds of the air have nests, but the Son of Man has nowhere to lay his head.'

He said to another man, 'Follow me.' But the man replied, 'Lord, first let me go and bury my father' . . .

Still another said, 'I will follow you, Lord; but first let me go back and say good-bye to my family.'

Jesus replied, 'No-one who puts his hand to the plough and looks back is fit for service in the kingdom of God.'

(Luke 9.57–62)

Interestingly in Matthew 8.19 it's a 'teacher of the law' who sparks off this dialogue by declaring that he'll follow Jesus wherever he goes. I wonder – did he? The law required Jews to be perfect. Some paid extraordinary attention to its every detail – and were always adding more codicils, inter-pretations and exacting requirements. A man could lose sight of God while trying to hang on to that lot, yet Jesus' 'yoke' – which means the requirements a rabbi put on his disciples – was 'light'. Or so he told them once, though it doesn't sound much like it from this passage.

Jesus' words are meant to be outrageous and we may well find ourselves spluttering at them. After all, 'honour-ing your father and mother' is not only one of the ten commandments; it would be considered morally good in most societies, along with providing a 'home' – physical and emotional support – for your family. In fact, Jesus was using the rabbinic technique of exaggeration to break through a prevailing mindset of perfectionism. And, after all, those who followed him everywhere for those three years had to leave jobs, homes – and risk their lives. I think Jesus was saying to them, 'Are you really prepared?'

He doesn't ask everyone to follow him in that way – whether in the first or twenty-first century, that would be absurd. Many of us are called to stay looking after our families in his name. Jesus summed up all ten commandments in just two when he answered another Jewish legal expert who asked, 'What must I do to inherit eternal life?' 'Love the Lord your God with all your heart and with all your soul and with all your strength and with all your mind'; and, 'Love your neighbour as yourself' (Luke 10.27). That's still requiring everything of us – but not through nit-picking detail, obsessive perfectionism, or unreasonable, punishing tasks. Had the teachers of the law been able to let go of their obsessive attention to detail, their perfectionism, maybe their hands and hearts would have had room to take hold of his love and shine it out for others.

Valerie Hunter, a retired bank clerk from Worthing, writes of how she let go of a different expression of perfectionism.

Have you ever noticed how quickly something new can become tarnished, damaged or spoilt? It happens to me all the time. I drop something greasy on a new article of clothing and it doesn't come clean again. As for my cherished new bicycle . . . It was a retirement present, really special. A pristine, sparkling machine. I'd not had a new bicycle for 40 years, so you can imagine my excitement.

Before long it fell against a concrete post. The crossbar dented, the paint was scratched and I was very upset and annoyed. For days the damage was the first thing I noticed and I almost let it spoil my rides.

These things don't matter to some but I have, until recently, strived to be a perfectionist in everything, worrying incessantly if a thing was not quite right. After I had a new front door fitted with a glass panel, it hit me in the eye every time I passed that the lines on its patterned squares didn't appear 100 per cent level. In the end I insisted that the glass be refitted. It did look better, to me anyway, but at what cost to others?

A perfectionist can't be easy to live with – and we cause anguish to ourselves, always scurrying around like busy mice, trying to put life and its contents in order, perfect order.

One day I learnt that Jesus is the only perfect one and that, although we can grow spiritually to be more like him, life on earth will never be perfect. So I let go of trying to have everything correct and faultless. I feel so much more at peace. When something new is spoilt it is a pity, but in the scale of life unimportant, as material things don't last. But God's love does. Jesus was the perfect sacrifice for our sins, our imperfections; our hope is of a perfect eternal life with him.

Jesus, I'm never going to live up to your two great commandments, let alone the more extreme demands which you place on some of your disciples. That's partly because I'm so easily distracted from letting your perfect love flow through me – by things like feeling smug about keeping certain moral codes while conveniently ignoring my conscience over others. Like Valerie, I can become distraught when I break or lose something, wasting hours, even days. Jesus, thank you that you give us your perfection in place of all our imperfections. Help each one of us to let go of anything which prevents our being motivated by your love, and from putting you first. Amen.

Letting go of obsessions

Bea Fishback writes about letting go of listening:

> Click . . . the second hand on the kitchen clock moves another notch. Click. The sound resembles a slow, dripping faucet. Click. Time seems to be standing still. Click. I'm trying to stop listening to the click, click, clicking.
>
> This morning I pulled the drapes aside and peered out at children waiting for their school bus. Their normal frenzied activities seemed frozen in space, like mannequins in a shop window, postures haphazard and free. Time is moving so slow. I need to let go of waiting.
>
> For him, time is irrelevant because he's surrounded by heightened sounds, unpredictability and anxious activity. He's hearing weapons, cries and foreign tongues. He's fighting a war while I'm surrounded by mundane normality. I need to let go of listening to television reports of casualties, to children arguing over who's sitting in the front of the car, or what to have for dinner. He's at war, while I'm fighting a battle of loneliness and fears.
>
> Click. What I want to hear is his voice, whispering sweet words in the darkness of our room, to feel his kiss on my cheek before his morning rush to work. Instead, I hear the clock clicking.
>
> Then, in between the click, click, click, I hear a still, small voice, a bit louder than the second hand. A soft, comforting sound whispers in the waiting space of my soul. 'After the fire the sound of a low whisper . . . And behold there came a voice to him and said, "What are you doing here, Elijah?"'

(1 Kings 19.12b, 13b, ESV). Good question! What am I doing, waiting, listening to the second hand, when I can let go and listen to God's voice instead? In a whisper, he comforts me with his presence. He takes away the mundane and gives me rest; he takes away my fears and gives his peace.

Lord, let me hear your holy whispers, instead of hollow clicking; tune my hearing to you and help me let go of the waiting.

Bea and her husband work on American Air Force bases throughout Europe, bringing spiritual and pastoral help to those who live there. Bea is particularly concerned for the wives left behind while their husbands serve in war zones. She knows what that is like because her husband was a serving officer for many years. I asked her to write something for this book about letting your loved ones go to work or fight abroad – and she sent me the piece above.

We feel so sorry for the woman in Bea's story. We identify – wouldn't we be the same, given similar circumstances? Perhaps we've had reason to be anxious about someone we love who is isolated from us and at risk – and we've found it hard to think about anything else. This woman has to endure months or years of that kind of pressure. If her obsessive thought pattern isn't broken, the stress will take its toll on her mental health and probably damage her family.

Bea wrote a women's Bible study, *Loving Your Military Man* (FamilyLife Publishing, 2007, available from <www.familylife.com> or <www.militaryministry.org>). It is based on Philippians 4.8. She speaks often on that passage, encouraging wives to focus on whatever is positive (God-type thinking) instead of mulling on the negative. While the Bible has little to say directly about obsession, it mentions our thought life often – that spring-fed pool which can become stagnant with 'hidden faults'.

Someone told me about the harbour at Caesarea, on the Mediterranean coast where the Romans engineered the world's first self-dredging harbour. It cleaned itself for 300 years, as the sea's natural currents daily washed any silt out through holes at the bottom of the harbour walls. When unhelpful thought patterns silt up our lives we may fear dredging – bringing the accumulated mud to the surface. But hasn't God provided ways in which the thoughts we harbour can dredge themselves, be washed out daily with the currents of his love, grace and goodness? Think on those things – and let the negative muck go!

You might like to meditate on the two passages below. Do we hold on to our negative thoughts? Or do we take them 'captive to Christ'? That's the quiet but desperate daily battle faced by those who have to let their loved ones go to war. Pray for them. Then ask God about any obsessive thoughts which, however 'understandable' in the circumstances, lead you away from Christ.

> Who can discern his errors? Forgive my hidden faults.
> Keep your servant also from wilful sins; may they not
>   rule over me. Then will I be blameless, innocent
>   of great transgression.
> May the words of my mouth and the meditation of my
>   heart be pleasing in your sight, O Lord, my Rock and
>   my Redeemer.
>
> (Psalm 19.12–14)

For though we live in the world, we do not wage war as the world does. The weapons we fight with are not the weapons of the world. On the contrary, they have divine power to demolish strongholds. We demolish arguments and every pretension that sets itself up against the knowledge of God, and we take captive every thought to make it obedient to Christ. (2 Corinthians 10.3–5)

Letting go of addictions

Alicia Arron writes:

The loft ladder emits its metallic shriek as I lower it segment by segment to the floor. I stand reluctant at the bottom, hesitating, unwilling. Knowing that resistance is impossible, I climb. I have to, there is no choice.

Holding tightly to the handrail, I enter the loft. It smells dank and dusty. The single, bare bulb illuminates every familiar case and box. The insulation in the slatted floor keeps the loft chilly and unwelcoming. I hate being there, powerless and alone with my guilt and fear.

Sitting on the floorboards I pick the lock of the battered weekend case. I had thrown away the key months previously in a futile attempt to prevent myself from reaching the contents, so now I lock and unlock it with a nail file. With a little patience it opens. There, nestling secretively in some old clothes, is my gin, the bottle half empty after my trip here an hour ago. This time I will finish the bottle. Then I might find some peace from the torment of addiction, the relentless craving to change the way I feel, and for sleep.

Feeling sick and dizzy I swig the contents neat. I don't enjoy it or want it, I just have to.

Descending the noisy, metal steps, I sigh with relief and slide the ladder back into the loft. Now all I have to do is get rid of the evidence – the empty bottle, camouflaged in a Tesco bag. I slide it noiselessly into a public waste bin. Then I can spend the day in a dull no-man's-land where nothing matters. I don't matter, nor do my life, my secrets, my lousy attempts at being a wife and mother.

For an hour or so the promise of the gin is reality. It doesn't last, it never does. The emotions, the craving come flooding back and the corner shop with its rows of shiny bottles draws me as it always does. I must have more.

That day was 20 years ago. Day after day I tried to find solace from my self-inflicted hell until finally the threat of losing my children made me ask for help. Once requested, it was given freely by other recovering alcoholics. Today I live without alcohol, secrets or addiction. My life is beyond my wildest dreams and the loft contains only memories.

Some things are very hard to understand. I've never been, never wanted to be, drunk enough to be ill. I've never wanted to smoke a cigarette, let alone take illegal drugs. That doesn't mean that I'm 'good' – simply that those particular things hold no allure for me.

I was 'addicted' to a particular solitaire game on the computer. After finishing some writing I'd have 'just one game' and find myself playing an hour later. Finding my inability to break the time-wasting habit disturbing, I asked my husband to remove the silly game from the computer. That solved the problem – so it was more a temporary obsession in my head than a full-blown addiction. I didn't try to sneak it back on, nor to play it at friends' houses. It did me no real harm and I've never played since. So what's the problem with letting go of real, harmful addictions? As Alicia's piece shows, soon they give no pleasure. Addicts know they will harm their health, finances, relationships, work – their whole life. Isn't it a no-brainer? Just give up. Remove the alcohol or other source of addiction and don't go near it again, dumbo! Alicia's story shows how it's not that simple. Such an uncompromising insight into what it is like to be an alcoholic moved me. I don't suppose anyone understands

alcoholism, fully. It may be a form of illness or genetic fault –
some experts talk of addictive personalities, others of addiction filling a huge gap in someone's life. Alicia believes it's a
threefold illness – mental, physical and spiritual.

My mild experience with solitaire wasn't a true addiction,
but helps me gain some insight that 'there but for the grace
of God . . .' To let go of a real addiction takes more than will-
power, more than hatred of its effects. Locks, keys, force,
magic pills, health professionals' skill, money – none of
these things give any guarantee of improvement. For Alicia,
the only way was through Alcoholics Anonymous which has
two million members across the world, all of them helping
to keep each other off alcohol. Through this remarkably
successful organization, Alicia has managed to turn her life
around and stay sober for 20 years.

The Bible has stories I don't understand, either. The
graphic description of a man's suffering in Mark 5.1–20
reminds me in some ways of Alicia's account of the controlling and destructive power which her addiction had over her.

> When Jesus got out of the boat, a man with an evil spirit
> came from the tombs to meet him. This man lived in the
> tombs, and no-one could bind him any more, not even with
> a chain. For he had often been chained hand and foot, but
> he tore the chains apart and broke the irons on his feet.
> No-one was strong enough to subdue him. Night and day
> among the tombs and in the hills he would cry out and cut
> himself with stones. (Mark 5.2–5)

The man had injured many and no one had been able to
help him, so he was kept in isolation, where he carried on
harming himself. We understand little enough today about

psychiatric illness; two thousand years ago they knew even less. It may well be that the 'demons' which tormented him emerged from the inner workings of a mind or personality which had become damaged – just as Alicia's 'demons' of alcoholism did. For peace and wholeness to be restored, both needed very special help.

In the Mark passage, Jesus had stilled a dangerous storm on Lake Galilee just before calming the demoniac. He went on to heal a woman who had haemorrhaged for 12 years, then raised Jairus' daughter. A pattern emerges. All the people involved had to let go of their devastating problem and trust Jesus. Then he showed his power – to calm, heal, set free, even snatch someone from the very jaws of death.

Alcoholics Anonymous, knowing that people cannot set themselves free, encourages them to look to 'a higher power' – anything you consider to be greater than yourself – the group, a loving God . . . for some it is Jesus. Other specifically Christian organizations are also successful in helping people who want to recover from addictions.

Lord, it is horrible when we see someone trapped in such unimaginable distress – more horrible for those who love them. May those with addictions or other destructive, controlling 'demons' find the strength and will to reach out for help to set them free.

Letting go of oppression

Fear made me stay. Fear of his threats, his deeds, his fingers of steel. I tried *everything* to keep him happy – like facing all the tins the same way and not phoning my parents.

He threw away our wedding presents; pulled me upstairs by my hair; threatened to kill me, several times.

I ran away twice. Once to an old school friend and once to a farm in Devon. Both times he found me and promised to change. Both times I believed him.

Fear clawed at my throat if the house was in darkness – in case he was hiding and ready to pounce. I was working for television and if I covered my costume designs from his critical gaze, he'd snort derision and pull my hand away. When I made his favourite supper, he'd throw it at the wall if I hadn't seasoned it exactly to his taste.

Gradually, Norris crushed joy from my life and replaced it with dread. It took me nearly six years to leave him. Encouraged by family and friends, finally I escaped with only the clothes that I was wearing.

My work blossomed and I found I could smile again. But I was constantly looking over my shoulder.

Incessant nightmares gave me years of waking in the night, drenched in sweat. It's OK, I'd tell myself. He's gone, maybe dead even.

I loved him once. Loved his piercing, green eyes and long, tapering fingers. Except those fingers could grab my flesh, squeezing until the pain made me gasp.

Then I met a gorgeous man. David asked me what I'd like to do on my fiftieth birthday.

'Lay a ghost,' I said. 'Please take me to the house, and let me see it with someone else living there. See a different car parked in the drive.'

Only there wasn't a different car. Just the same one I'd driven 24 years ago. And tinkering under the bonnet was my ex-husband. My legs turned to jelly and my hammering heart told me I was as much in fear as ever.

Suddenly, I knew what to do. 'I need to go in alone,' I said to David.

'I'll worry about you.'

'I'll be fine.' Taking a deep breath, I pushed open the iron gates. The screech of metal made Norris look up. As his mouth formed an 'O', I realized I had the upper hand.

'Christ! What're you doing here?'

'Laying a ghost.'

I only stayed ten minutes, but from that moment on, the nightmares stopped. I didn't look over my shoulder any more. I started drawing again and wore silly clothes.

And I dyed my hair pink.

My costume-designer friend Josephine is one of the kindest, loveliest people I know. She married Norris very young, very innocent. I met her when she was in her late fifties and everything she's written about above had already happened. She was blissfully happy with David, creative in her home and work, looking wonderful with her pink hair and fantastic clothes. Always helping her family and others, full of both compassion and fun – Josephine was a very 'together' person, living an enviable life. Even so, in our creative-writing classes she would often write about those oppressive years with her first husband – perhaps because the turning point of that brief visit to him had finally freed her to do that. Josephine made me realize how, long after it is over, the effects of oppression can last. Often people let go of any confidence and hold on to fear decades after the source of their oppression is removed.

That takes us to the heart of Jesus' message of freedom. He came declaring much the same message as God told Moses to declare to the oppressive Pharaoh in Egypt, 'Let my people go.' Most of the people who heard Jesus assumed that, as Messiah, he'd been appointed by God to free them from their violent Roman occupiers – and as a consequence also from the oppression of extreme poverty. Is it surprising they interpreted his 'manifesto' in this way?

> He went to Nazareth, where he had been brought up, and on the Sabbath day he went into the synagogue, as was his custom. And he stood up to read. The scroll of the prophet Isaiah was handed to him. Unrolling it, he found the place where it is written:
>
> 'The Spirit of the Lord is on me, because he has anointed me to preach good news to the poor. He has sent me to proclaim freedom for the prisoners and recovery of sight for the blind, to release the oppressed, to proclaim the year of the Lord's favour.'
>
> Then he rolled up the scroll, gave it back to the attendant and sat down. The eyes of everyone in the synagogue were fastened on him, and he began by saying to them, 'Today this scripture is fulfilled in your hearing.'   (Luke 4.16–21)

In what way was that Scripture 'fulfilled' that day? Jesus didn't defeat the Romans then, nor later in his life on earth. Instead they crucified him. Far from releasing others from poverty, Jesus ended up with no possessions himself, apart from a robe – and even that was taken from him. How could his followers hold on, now that all hope had vanished?

Yet hold on they did – and went forward to face oppression, poverty and death undaunted. If you have time, read the story of Stephen in Acts 6 and 7. Those early followers, like many since, found Jesus' resurrected power did indeed save them from the effects of oppression at the most fundamental level. As 2 Timothy 1.7–8 says:

> For God did not give us a spirit of timidity, but a spirit of power, of love and of self-discipline. So do not be ashamed to testify about our Lord, or ashamed of me his prisoner. But

join with me in suffering for the gospel, by the power of
God.

Herod, then the Romans, did fall, as do all oppressive
regimes, eventually. Slavery took far longer – and still
flourishes in many places. Jesus himself said, 'The poor
will always be with you.' So on a physical level, 'Let my
oppressed people go' wasn't working. Doesn't God care
about that? Is the freedom from oppression that he offers
purely spiritual? No. God's rule is never oppressive; his
heart, as exposed on almost every page of the Bible, beats
for the freedom of those who are oppressed.

As we pray, 'Your kingdom come on earth as it is in
heaven', we're to do everything we can against poverty and
oppression. That includes the often-hidden oppression of
domestic violence. Here are some statistics from the UK. One
in four women will suffer it at some time during their lives
and it accounts for almost a quarter of all recorded crime.
Half of all women murdered are killed by a partner – that's
between one and two per week. And I'm told by counsellors
that violence within marriage is equally prevalent among
Christians and non-believers. It's more common among
the clergy than lay members of churches, where a clergyman
is responsible for running the church alone. He takes his
frustrations out on his wife in the privacy of their 'tied'
home – which she will lose if she reports him.

Lord, most of the people I know are so kind they wouldn't
oppress a fly, so violence within the supposedly loving commitment of marriage shocks me – especially if it happens
among Christians! Help me and all of us to be aware. Help
us to let go of our natural spirit of timidity and, when we

see oppression in any form, to challenge it in your spirit of love, power and self-control. And give all those who have suffered oppression the courage to let go of its effects and find true freedom again.

Letting go of hurtful attitudes, holding on to love

Get rid of all bitterness, rage and anger, brawling and slander, along with every form of malice. Be kind and compassionate to one another, forgiving each other, just as in Christ God forgave you. (Ephesians 4.31–32)

Rid yourselves of all such things as these: anger, rage, malice, slander and filthy language from your lips. Do not lie to each other, since you have taken off your old self with its practices and have put on the new self, which is being renewed in knowledge in the image of its Creator.

(Colossians 3.8–10)

Why is it so easy to hold on to things like anger, bitterness, jealousy, hatred and lies? They do us no good at all but can make us so stressed that we become ill. How much better to let them go and hold on instead to kindness, compassion, love – everything which God seeded in us and longs to see grow.

Marian Foss joined my writing group a few years ago. Though her mother is involved in her local church I'm not sure that Marian would claim to be a Christian, yet her story is full of redemption, of the way of Jesus – which so often differs from our own human way. Here she tells it herself:

I realized that it was time to let go of the anger and bitterness I had held on to for so many years. I don't know where it all started but, by the time I had reached my teens, I'd grown to hate my mother with a vengeance. I couldn't wait to leave home and go to college. After that we drifted apart. She would phone me often but I'd be reduced to instant anger at the sound of her voice.

Life went on the same. I held on to my anger. She continued to ring me and be caring and solicitous. What did she want with me? I had no idea. I wasn't nice but morose, hating the family get-togethers that punctuated my year. I worked hard. I worked hard at my relationships. It didn't occur to me to improve this one.

Surprising how changes can occur quickly, or else sneak up on you. Mine came through an extraordinary situation. Much to my annoyance, at the wrong time, with the wrong person, I fell in love.

Nothing went smoothly in this decidedly one-sided love affair. I was never sure what he made of me but I was determined to extract good out of something which had changed my life. Things didn't improve. He rejected me terribly. Determining to find the solution, I went to bed. Early onset arthritis was crippling me anyway. I was adamant that I'd stay in bed until I had found out the solution.

I saw me loving him and I saw him disliking me. Then I thought – what does this remind me of, what situation? I was so slow, so stupid. At last I saw – my mother and me – the relationship we had shared for years. Then I saw something vital that I'd missed before. I'd always seen my mother's love as weakness. Fancy loving a person who only hurts and despises you! Then it came to me. It was love that was the strength. Being hurtful and angry, that was the weakness.

So I got out of bed, into my car, drove to my mother's home and did the most difficult thing I have ever done. Told her that I loved her.

Letting my anger go wasn't easy. It didn't happen all at once but over time I worked at it. I bought books on emotions. I learnt about the games we play and how we hurt each other. Then I learnt to put things right.

Things have changed over the last few years. It is hard to imagine how much, now that we share a home together. The other night I was out with friends and said to one of them, 'Living with my mother has actually made me a better person.'

'You ought to tell her,' said the friend. But I don't think I need to. She knows.

Marian's change of heart took effort and a willingness to examine parts of herself that seemed dark. But it was worth it! She wrote this poem which reminds me of a stunning natural history documentary in which explorers descended for several days' journey into the darkest depths of a remote cave, to find themselves surrounded by 'rooms' of the most amazing white crystals which sparkled in their lamplight – something seen by only a handful of people previously.

> Into the darkness
> Hand over foot,
> Foot over hand,
> Down and down.
>
> Into the cave,
> Bats fly around me.
> Holding on to the rope
> Dangling, hanging.
>
> Then I look down
> Into the cavern
> Lit up with lights
> Like a Christmas dream.

Rock upon rock,
Sparkling like sapphires.
Hanging and dangling
In the abyss.

Proverbs 14.30 says, 'A heart at peace gives life to the body, but envy rots the bones.' Ask God about any area where your heart is not at peace. Are you holding on to some bad attitudes which may even have consequences for your physical health? Or do you know of others whose relationships have become poisonous? Could you be a peacemaker?

Letting go of bitterness, holding on to forgiveness

Then Peter came to Jesus and asked, 'Lord, how many times shall I forgive my brother when he sins against me? Up to seven times?'

Jesus answered, 'I tell you, not seven times, but seventy-seven times.' (Matthew 18.21–22)

Therefore I tell you, whatever you ask for in prayer, believe that you have received it, and it will be yours. And when you stand praying, if you hold anything against anyone, forgive him, so that your Father in heaven may forgive you your sins. (Mark 11.24–25)

Yesterday an item on the news sickened me. Ten or twelve youths had gang-raped a teenage girl with learning difficulties and then doused her in caustic soda. She remains severely traumatized and her skin is so damaged that she can't even control her own body temperature. Some of the gang were found guilty and given – it seemed to me – insufficient jail terms. I was thinking – what they did is unforgivable.

And so it is, by me, as I don't know the perpetrators, nor the victim. I can pray for all involved. I can say that the deed was utterly evil but I have no right either to take revenge or to release those men from retribution. Jesus' words about those people who sin against *us* though, are uncompromising. How would I react if someone did something terrible to me or to someone I love?

I remember another news item – not the details but the way it moved me. A woman, through her tears, was saying she forgave the killers of her young, innocent son and was even praying for them. 'How? Why?' the reporter asked in astonishment. How – by the grace of God. Why – because, if she did anything else, she and the rest of the family would be destroyed by bitterness. So said the mother. And she was right.

Hebrews 12.15 says, 'See to it that no-one misses the grace of God and that no bitter root grows up to cause trouble and defile many.' History shows repeated damage to whole families, communities, even nations when people hold on to bitterness and revenge, while rejecting any idea of forgiveness and redemption.

That grieving mother – a black Christian, like her murdered son – had found the grace of God to forgive, to let go of any desire for vengeance, even to pray for redemption for her son's killers. The spate of killings, of which her son was but one victim, were utterly wrong. If they were going to stop, she knew it wasn't through hitting back – only by God's grace and redemption. We can only hope to find the grace to forgive because he first forgave us, even though we killed his Son, who in his turn forgave his killers. A cycle of redemption like that has to be better than a vendetta.

Letting go of the bad, holding on to the good

Jesus taught us to pray: 'Forgive us our debts, as we also have forgiven our debtors' (Matthew 6.12). But what if we're in debt, through no fault of our own, and our creditors won't forgive us?

Young Freda Evans went to work on a farm, fell in love with it – and with the farmer. Soon they were married and all went pretty well for 30 years, until he died in August 1992. Freda takes up the story of what happened next:

Following my husband's death, I struggled for four months to keep the staff and farm running smoothly. Then I received the ultimate Christmas present. Delivered in true Santa-style by recorded delivery on Christmas Eve, it informed me that my husband's brother Steve was beginning a high court action to evict me from the farm with as little notice as possible.

I knew this would happen if my husband predeceased his brother, as they were tenants-in-common and I was not on the tenancy. The speed and venom with which it was done stunned me. Steve's casual remark on Christmas morning of 'I'd better not wish you a happy Christmas in the circumstances!' proved the icing on the cake.

We had a traditional mixed farm – arable with grazing, some 300 sheep, 120 milking cows plus beef and young stock. Many of the cattle were in calf and all the sheep were in lamb. There are only certain times in a cow's lactation when it is possible to sell her to advantage, and the middle of winter is not one of them. Steve wanted them all slaughtered, which was anathema to me. I refused to slaughter any that were in calf and pleaded their case before the judge. Having bred and reared all stock for the previous 30 years, I couldn't condemn them to such an end. I was allowed time to bring them to a suitable stage, then sell them. Many young in-calf heifers went to a young couple beginning their farming dream, who kindly kept in touch about the progress of at least some of my stock.

It proved a long-drawn-out affair before I was finally evicted from the farm and my home of 33 years. All through the court battles I'd prayed for Steve and his family. As a Christian I knew that was right and the only way to prevent bitterness and revenge in myself. Many times during those two years of umpteen solicitors' letters and court appearances I spilled over with anger and the desire for vengeance. But I kept making the hard choice not to go down that road.

Because of all the farm debts, my accountant suggested bankruptcy as the easiest option – after all, I had nothing. But I chose to take the honourable route and several years later he was amazed when, by the grace of God, I paid them all off.

Lord, you know how hard we find forgiveness. When we do reach a place where we're able to let go of our desire for revenge on the person who has hurt us and to pray for their redemption, it becomes a daily decision, a daily battle. So you, Lord, who keeps forgiving us every day for the fresh wrongs we do, you who choose not to remember the way we hurt you in the past – show us how; give us your strength and grace. Amen.

Letting go of worry, holding on to trust

Alexine Crawford runs a bed-and-breakfast, and works with a charity for disabled people. With children serving the Lord around the world, she has had to learn about how to let go of worry and hand it over to God. She writes:

'I am sending you out as lambs among wolves,' we heard as the church blessed our son Dickon and his family on their way to Mozambique. My heart gave a lurch. Wolves? I knew that Mozambique was littered with unexploded landmines. But wolves! I tried not to imagine my beautiful little granddaughter being maimed by either. All we could do was to entrust the family to God.

It wasn't the first such parting. Ten years earlier Dickon went to work with VSO in Nepal, the world's only officially Hindu nation. There he lived in primitive conditions working with local foresters. To reach that outpost there was first a flight in a little plane which landed on a mountain plateau, then a choice between a bus driven wildly along vertiginous roads or a long walk.

Meanwhile Clare, his long-time girlfriend, followed a call from God to supervise a mission farm in Mozambique. I wept saying goodbye to her, for how could the two of them ever now be together? Again, all I could say was 'Over to you, God' and pray affirming that he had it all in hand.

When Dickon and Clare eventually did marry, they went to Nepal for four years with Tearfund. And then came the call back to Mozambique and the alarming commission.

I suppose I could have tormented myself with worrying about them, but what would that have achieved? We heard about their scary moments only after they had happened.

One evening Clare drove with their two children to meet Dickon, who was due to arrive in a small plane on the local unlit airstrip. As the dusk thickened she was thinking the pilot must have decided it was too late in the day to make the journey when she saw the plane approaching. Terrified, she knew at once that it was going to overshoot. She watched it land and slew round through 90 degrees. It had been halted by trenches dug to remove landmines and was badly damaged, but the passengers emerged unscathed.

Statistically, more missionaries die through travel accidents than from any other cause, and of course their modes of transport are often hazardous.

And what about illness? Dickon and Clare took our grandson Jonathan to Mozambique when he was four weeks old. One could worry about a catalogue of tropical illnesses, and missionary societies are realistic about the possibility of death. But our children have made their choice, and we have had to release them to fulfil it.

For me to worry after the event, or about future events, only puts an added burden on them, and on me. And when I have prayed about a worry, I remind myself to thank God that I can leave it with him.

(A version of this story was first published
in *Woman Alive*)

Most of us, like Alexine, learn because we're always being challenged about worry. The alternative is stress, sleepless nights or even physical illness. How much easier if Jesus promised to keep all who serve him safe from harm – yet clearly his first followers, and many since, have been killed because of their faith in him. Jesus said:

I am sending you out like sheep among wolves. Therefore be as shrewd as snakes and as innocent as doves. Be on your guard against men; they will hand you over to the local councils and flog you in their synagogues. On my account you will be brought before governors and kings as witnesses to them and to the Gentiles. But when they arrest you, do not worry about what to say or how to say it. At that time you will be given what to say, for it will not be you speaking, but the Spirit of your Father speaking through you.

(Matthew 10.16–20)

If you're honest, don't the words, 'when they arrest you' or 'when you are persecuted' cause you to gulp at the exhortation not to worry or fear? We can't accuse Jesus, or the missionary society in Alexine's story, of hiding or minimizing considerable dangers. But however big or small, real or imagined, the source of our worry turns out to be, Jesus is right. Our anxiety can only make it worse.

He said: 'Do not worry about tomorrow, for tomorrow will worry about itself. Each day has enough trouble of its own' (Matthew 6.34). If I use up all my energy today in worrying about tomorrow, then if the troubles arrive tomorrow and I haven't slept or eaten, I'm not going to have the resources to deal with them. There's nothing wrong with forward planning but worrying ahead is daft when you stop to think about it. So is worrying about someone else when there's nothing we can do to help.

Again, Jesus is very practical when he asks, 'Who of you by worrying can add a single hour to his life?' (Matthew 6.27). How many hours are lost to worry – useful hours that we could be enjoying? If we let go of all that worry then we might enjoy a longer lifespan too. If we could let go . . . but how?

Jesus' words which follow today's Bible passage aren't very comforting. 'Do not be afraid of those who kill the body but cannot kill the soul. Rather, be afraid of the one who can destroy both soul and body in hell' (Matthew 10.28). Great, so now we're worrying about God and eternity as well as everything else! But he goes on to say:

> Are not two sparrows sold for a penny? Yet not one of them will fall to the ground apart from the will of your Father.

And even the very hairs of your head are all numbered. So
don't be afraid; you are worth more than many sparrows.

(Matthew 10.29–31)

Fear and worry have hold over us when we give them our full
attention. If we give that instead to God – who loves each
one of us enough to number the hairs on our heads – then
fear starts to lose its grip. Our perspective has changed. If
worship means 'to give worth to' then we can choose to
'worship' fear and worry, believing that they are stronger
than anything – or we can choose to worship God by giving him our full attention and by believing that he really does
know and love us.

Lord, for all of us who find it hard to let go of our anxieties,
whether or not we have anything realistic to worry about,
help us! Help us to see things from your perspective. Help
us to worship you in spirit and in truth by truly putting you
before all our worries. Help us to hold on to you!

Letting go of sin, holding on to our new life in Christ

We died to sin; how can we live in it any longer? . . . buried
with him through baptism into death in order that, just
as Christ was raised from the dead through the glory of the
Father, we too may live a new life . . . The death he died, he
died to sin once for all; but the life he lives, he lives to God.
In the same way, count yourselves dead to sin but alive to
God in Christ Jesus. Therefore do not let sin reign in your
mortal body so that you obey its evil desires . . . rather offer
yourselves to God, as those who have been brought from

54

death to life . . . as instruments of righteousness. For sin shall not be your master, because you are not under law, but under grace.   (Romans 6.2–14)

Paul makes it sound so cut and dried, doesn't he? Let go of sin and live rightly by the resurrection power of Jesus – simple. But the closer I come to Jesus the more I realize how far his right living is immeasurably better than mine. Using Paul's picture of baptism – 'seeing myself' as dead and then raised to the sinless vibrancy of Christ's life – frankly doesn't help me much. But one of our church's ministers, Steve Elmes, showed me how all this might work and has given me permission to draw from his sermon here.

First he asked us to imagine that a man moves to a different house in a different town. Three months later, finding that he still has the key to the back door, he returns to his former home, lets himself in, helps himself to food from the fridge and settles down in the lounge to watch TV. When the new owners return they say, quite rightly, 'What on earth are you doing here? This is no longer your house. Go away!' Just so, for Christians, habitual sin is no longer our territory. We don't belong there.

I reflected that not everything changes so quickly. I once ghostwrote a book for Philippa Stroud about her work with homeless people. When they became Christians, dramatic, almost miraculous changes would often happen. Swearing, violence or drunkenness might stop overnight – but it would take patient months and years to help people let go of other aspects of their chaotic, sinful lives. With Christ there is hope, a new start, a real chance to change – and a promise that sin need no longer be our master. But we have a part to play – it doesn't work without our co-operation.

Steve illustrated this with a story of when his Apple Mac crashed. The logic board had gone and would cost £500 to replace. Initially dismayed, Steve remembered that he paid into the 'Apple care plan'. He had to 'activate' his cover by keying in his password – but would the scheme work in practice? Yes! With joy he discovered that the whole cost really was covered. Just so, he said, when we struggle with a besetting sin, we can't do it on our own but we can 'activate' Christ's power at work within us. 'It's not some fiction or vague comfort,' he said. 'It really works.' He went on to tell the following story.

Lately I've been struggling. Suffice it to say that my days have been fearful – dogged by a sense of foreboding. I've found myself becoming angry, thinking unkind things, sometimes even acting upon them. I didn't like what I was seeing in myself. I tried to pray, on my own and with others, but seemed unable to move out of this state.

Eventually I found myself asking the Lord, 'Does this Christianity really work? Because it doesn't seem to work for me right now. I feel stuck.'

Then, last Sunday, I was preaching at another church. During the service I had a picture of someone bound around the neck and shoulders and sensed the Lord saying, 'I am the God who sets people free from fear, shame and guilt.'

I passed this on to the congregation and then a woman told us of God's strange-sounding word to her a few weeks previously, before she'd been healed of immobility in her neck and shoulders: 'Why do you doubt my love?' I responded to her story of God's love bringing freedom – and at the end of the service felt God prompting me to ask her for prayer. As she prayed I seemed to hear the words, 'Stand up', and at the same time felt my body straighten. I took it as a sign that the promise had been activated – that

I was now able to stand tall and to live uprightly in Christ's power and love.

My gloom, fear, anger, edginess – all of them lifted and disappeared and in the days that have followed I've lived with a sense of release. I've known God's power as available to me, so that I can respond to his call to live uprightly, standing tall. God's love has ministered to me at a deeper level, enabling me to respond and to live this new life that Paul writes about. That's not to say I've not had any struggles since that prayer. I would not want to give an unrealistic picture. Yet I am convinced within of the truth of Paul's words in Romans 6 – we have a new life in Christ and God's power is at work to actualize the change as we co-operate with him.

Lord, sometimes you put your finger on a sinful area in our lives and we know we need to let go of it, to change, to move out of the old house and live in your new one. Help us then to remember that, though we can't do it in our own strength, we can activate yours!

Thank you for great resources – including the ministry of the body of Christ on earth. Help us to activate them and to live in the freedom of the new life which Jesus won for us.

Letting go of guilt, holding on to relationship

The LORD is compassionate and gracious, slow to anger, abounding in love. He will not always accuse, nor will he harbour his anger for ever; he does not treat us as our sins deserve or repay us according to our iniquities.

For as high as the heavens are above the earth, so great is his love for those who fear him; as far as the east is from the west, so far has he removed our transgressions from us.

> As a father has compassion on his children, so the LORD
> has compassion on those who fear him; for he knows how
> we are formed, he remembers that we are dust . . .
>
> But from everlasting to everlasting the LORD's love is
> with those who fear him, and his righteousness with their
> children's children – with those who keep his covenant and
> remember to obey his precepts.   (Psalm 103.8–18)

God certainly knows how to let go in forgiveness! Under the
old covenant, he moved transgressions away 'as far as the
east is from the west'. He chooses not to remember our sins,
though they have broken the very spirit and basis of our relationship with him, as well as the 'legal' side of our covenant.
Isaiah 43.24–25 says: 'You have burdened me with your
sins and wearied me with your offences. I, even I, am he who
blots out your transgressions, for my own sake, and remembers your sins no more.' In that particular instance
the people hadn't even called upon him, nor made any of
the sacrifices required to deal with sin before Jesus came to
do that once and for all. They had let go, yet God was still
'holding on' to them, holding on to his side of the agreement.

His grace in 'holding on' and 'letting go' at just the right
times is extraordinary. We are not so good at those things!
Most of us wander off sometimes, letting the relationship
which we have with him go, just when we should be holding on. But then, when we've been forgiven, we hold on to
our guilt, letting it poison both us and other people, despite
the fact that Jesus already drank that poison for us on the
cross. He took the vinegar – the bitterness and pain of it
all – and, although the consequences of our sin may live on,
we need to know that the consequences of our guilt could
die with him, if we'd only give it to him and let it go. Then
we could 'rise with him' to a real newness of life.

Letting go of the bad, holding on to the good

This is illustrated so well by Margaret MacKenzie's story:

I suppose I knew very early on that my marriage was a mistake. We were so unsuited – why hadn't I seen that? However, a year or so down the line, two children made a difference. I still felt we were wrong together, yet loyalty and a desire to preserve the family unit kept me with him. Eventually, though, I'd no qualms about having 'a friend' – which kept me sane for a few years, until my 'friend' found someone else. I reached such a state of anger, jealousy and hatred that everything began to turn inward, destroying what little self-confidence I had. Trying to carry on as normal while covering up my depression became more and more difficult.

One day, a very good real friend took me in hand and persuaded me to let go of all my anger and resentment. I hadn't been a Christian but she said I could turn to God and ask his forgiveness for all my sins and that he would help me to have a future. Then began a very hard, long struggle to deal with all my feelings of self-hatred, frustration, shame and rejection – to say nothing of self-pity.

I did become a Christian in time and it meant my husband and I were able to rub along together fairly amicably. I set about helping him get on top of his debts.

After a year or so my husband died without much warning and my life changed dramatically. I suddenly realized after a while that I was happier than I had ever been and felt my God had given me this chance to find myself. I was sorry that it was at the expense of my husband's life as he was a nice man, even though we had irreconcilable differences.

Now, living alone, I have found such peace and joy in my Lord and Saviour, Jesus Christ. I know that he has not only forgiven but forgotten my sins and all I ask now is to be his hands and feet in this world until he calls me home.

Who is a God like you, who pardons sin and forgives the transgression of the remnant of his inheritance? You do not stay angry for ever but delight to show mercy. You will again have compassion on us; you will tread our sins underfoot and hurl all our iniquities into the depths of the sea.

(Micah 7.18–19)

If we claim to be without sin, we deceive ourselves and the truth is not in us. If we confess our sins, he is faithful and just and will forgive us our sins and purify us from all unrighteousness. (1 John 1.8–9)

Letting go of fear, holding on to trust

It is I; don't be afraid. (John 6.20)

I looked up 'fear' in the Bible concordance. Nine out of ten references were to fearing the Lord – not what I sought. So I looked up 'afraid' – ah, pages of that. Presumably, since most of us are fearful, we need reminding often not to be afraid. God knows how hard it is for us to let go of fear.

Here's a thought. Being afraid is passive – it's a state, like 'I am hungry'. Fearing is active – we take control and decide to fear, as we might decide to refrain from food ('I fear' and 'I fast' are active verbs). Sometimes it's good to fear – it stops us walking too near to cliff edges. Living in a constant state of anxiety, though, is clearly not good.

So, when we start to fear and then reach a state of being afraid, where fear is part of our identity, how do we become free? Maybe we need something to replace fear's power, for example by cultivating the fear of the Lord – putting that above our feelings of being afraid. We need to acknowledge that he has all the power – he could crush us, along with everything which we fear. But he's also Love and has promised not to crush us. The Bible says: 'Fear the Lord' but in the Bible verse quoted above, when Jesus is walking across the stormy sea towards the understandably terrified disciples, he says: 'It is I; don't be afraid.'

I was talking after church to a lovely Christian woman who wakes every morning with fear weighing her down and knotting her stomach. Her fears, rooted in her childhood, have prevented her from doing so much – but little by little the Holy Spirit is freeing her. She'd just had another breakthrough; her face was shining. 'This week I felt Jesus plant something new inside of me and it's growing, pushing the fear away. I'm beginning to believe that I can do some of the things I've been asked to do, without being so afraid that I'll mess up!'

Fear's grip is powerful. But faith, trust and love are stronger. If we can't let go of being afraid and hold on to them, in the person of Jesus, then his faith, trust and love will hold on to us.

Dr Sharman Jeffries, research psychologist and mentor, tells us how she can now let go of fear, rather than being always afraid.

I am writing this in a cubicle, waiting to be processed for a minor operation in an hour's time. I have signed the consent form, been warned of possible dangers – necessary but a little alarming. I am not fearful in an emotional sense but my heart rate is raised slightly: my body is reacting to the sounds, the place and to my helplessness. I am putting my trust in the anaesthetist and surgeon's skill – and in God, who knows all about me and my situation.

In contrast, I remember fainting with fear in A&E while waiting for an assessment of a dodgy knee, convinced it was a DVT or something terminal. My heart rate soared, my head throbbed with the beats, sweat filmed my hands and brow, my legs began to tremble and I was drifting away somewhere ... anywhere ... A perceptive consultant saw my distress, held my hand and explained exactly what was going on in my body. Then he asked me about my situation: on my own with two little girls and no money if I couldn't drive to work. He said, 'I believe your knee will get better when things change for the better for you.' I calmed down. And he was right, it did.

From a young age I'd had to be independent. When growing up I never learnt to let go of fear, deal with anxiety or to trust in people – and never saw others doing those things. Over the years, I have learnt to trust myself to others, and have found by experience that most people (and God) are for me, not against me.

I can still feel fearful as I stand up in our worship band to play and sing, even though I have practised as much as I can – hands a little sweaty and shaky, stomach churning. 'Will I do OK? Help people to worship? Or will I really mess up?' Now I've learnt that those feelings are not helpful – they do not always tell me the truth. I offer what I have as best I can. The rest is not up to me.

Whether waiting for an operation or waiting to perform, I've learnt how to deal with the fear and leave the outcome with the Lord. I remember my daughter telling me she had learnt something vitally important to her: 'I do what I can; God does what I can't.' It became important for me too: it's my way of letting go of my fears.

Jesus, do what we can't. Take our fears. Help us to see you as you are, standing in front of us, saying: 'It is I: don't be afraid.'

Letting go of misunderstanding, embracing truth

Andy Parr, a senior project analyst from Bromsgrove, writes:

The snapshot is of you, given to me by your sister when I came looking, only to find that you had gone. That snapshot looks like me, in a dress, which is disconcerting and makes me wonder. Were you ugly or was I pretty, for a boy?

Reconciling memories with dreams is strange when you have dreamed those memories all your life. I dreamt so long about why my fate was to be adopted. My memories were not truth as, like that snapshot taken long ago, they captured a transient moment as though it were something still and constant. I wondered, could my whole life be a construct of my mind? I could construct a story but where did it end and my memory start?

I am tied by law to Mum and Dad, my adoptive parents who did their best to care, even to replace the love of the mother tied to me by blood, who gave me up. But I didn't know for myself what that kind of love was all about until my first son was born. I loved him and understood for the first time what it means to have a connection by means of blood. That's when I started looking for you.

I found you too late . . . was it too late? You'd been dead for just six months. I talked with your sister. She gave me that snapshot. I have a story now of who you were, why you had me, and why you kept that secret all your life.

Until I had a child of my own I didn't care, I didn't know. On becoming a father I realized how much you cared and had to lose by giving me up so that I could choose a life and a path which you could not provide. I didn't know, I got it wrong, how much you cared when you let go – how you thought it would be best for me to have the care of a mum and dad, a care that you could not deliver.

I hope you knew before you died that I forgave you and was reconciled to a better memory than at first I had. I hope that in your dreams I turned out happy, loved and cherished – that you knew what you did was for the best. I hope you found God's peace as the denial you carried all your life was unburdened before the end and that you knew some day I would seek you out and remember you fondly, understanding how you tried to do right for me, bearing the cost and pain all your life so that I didn't have to. Whatever were the misunderstandings they no longer matter because I know I am loved and can hold on to that as a truth.

There is a part of me that wishes we'd met and yet that same part holds you as a memory and knows that we didn't meet for a reason – perhaps it was all in the Lord's timing that we never spoke. I wonder whether it would have been too much to see me again when you'd become reconciled to having lost me? I often think that God knew it was too much for us to bear to have been part of each other's lives and so left us both with memories of each other – the people we'd never met since first we parted.

Who are you? Where do you come from, in terms of genes as well as geography and culture? Who loves ya, baby? Who doesn't? And why? Such fundamental questions, left un-answered, can affect people at the deepest level, even if at first they don't realize that they care. Andy told me that he went through some difficult times in his youth, years before his own son's birth became the catalyst which impelled him to find and understand his birth mother.

The four Gospels devote a lot of space to Jesus confront-ing the fundamental misunderstandings which even his own followers had about his identity, teaching, morality, standing with God and so on. Here is one snippet:

Letting go of the bad, holding on to the good

To the Jews who had believed him, Jesus said, 'If you hold to my teaching, you are really my disciples. Then you will know the truth, and the truth will set you free.'

They answered him, 'We are Abraham's descendants and have never been slaves of anyone. How can you say that we shall be set free?'

Jesus replied, 'I tell you the truth, everyone who sins is a slave to sin. Now a slave has no permanent place in the family, but a son belongs to it for ever. So if the Son sets you free, you will be free indeed.'   (John 8.31–36)

Jesus came and changed the whole picture of life, the universe and everything – perhaps most fundamentally because no one previously had enjoyed anything like the quality of relationship which he had with his Father. He swept away generations of misunderstandings of 'family history' to reopen humanity's path to that love which had always been meant for all of us.

So . . . who are we? Not people trying to be good or claiming descent from some spiritual leader; we're children of God! Where do we come from? From our parents' genes, yes, but more importantly from our Creator and Redeemer. Who loves us? Father God, Jesus, the Holy Spirit, the other children in his family . . . 'His own did not receive him. Yet to all who received him, to those who believed in his name, he gave the right to become children of God' (John 1.11b–12).

Thank God that you are loved, hold on to that as truth and let his love take its own time to soak away all the pain and shame of your human misunderstandings, whether petty or fundamental.

Holding on or letting go – in life

———◆———

On the edge – of letting go or holding on

Teacher Julia Jarrett describes very well in this poem what it is like to suffer from vertigo when standing near the edge of a high building – on this occasion in Kew Gardens.

Vertigo at the Pagoda
Melting parts of me ooze
towards the window.
I can't hold it back.
Liquid limbs of my mind
tremble to
look at the cedars below me.
Being this giant terrifies me.
My feet turn to drizzle
trickling towards the edge
of the stairs.
The banister shrinks.
Tears pull me to the stairs' void.
Yellow creeps up my spine
into my face to dissolve me
downwards.

Nikki Slater, a member of my church, is National Training Manager for Anchor Staying Put, which offers services enabling elderly people in England to stay in their own homes. Nikki doesn't suffer from physical vertigo but has experienced what it is like to be pulled to the edge, in more ways than one. She writes:

> Looking back, there was nothing in my life that particularly caused my behaviour to be the way it was. But I was never happy and I really didn't ever know why. My life went from broken friendship to better jobs to loads of money and possessions, then through a husband and many affairs, eventually settling into a relationship with a man who gave me all the attention I craved but abused me both mentally and physically. I knew I was on the verge of a breakdown and could almost see it happening in slow motion. I hated everything I was, everything I had and everything I might have been. I'd lied, cheated, stolen and couldn't see a way out of my situation.
>
> So one night in February 2002, after crying wolf to get attention on a few occasions by saying I wanted to kill myself, I made the ultimate decision.
>
> Talking about suicide and actually preparing for it are two totally different things. When you've decided to let go and know you have about an hour left to live, there aren't any words that could describe how rejected and desperate you feel, nor how committed you are to end the mess you're in.
>
> So I drove my car nine miles from where I used to live to Beachy Head, a local beauty spot well known for its life-ending cliff. Still dressed in my pyjamas and dressing gown, I parked. I got out, crossed the road and walked to the edge. I remember standing on the sign that warned you it was dangerous to get any closer. I had every intention of letting go.
>
> And then I heard *him*. I heard my name and I felt a firm touch on my chest and an overwhelming sense of love and happiness like I'd never experienced before. He said,

'Nikki, I love you.' I knew that I had a choice – I could let go if I chose to do so. But I knew also – in my soul, my heart and every sinew of me – that if I chose to hold on, which was what the voice wanted me to do, he would be with me for ever.

So I chose to hold on and in a funny way I then let go of all the bad stuff in my past – the insecurities, loneliness, desperation and hopelessness that I felt towards living. I understood that letting go of my self-hatred, my belief that I didn't need help, my bad past and my unknown future meant that I had something – and more importantly some-*one* – to hold on to, every day of my life for all the years since then. I still have trials and I still rely on hearing that same voice to enable me to hold on, but I'll never let go again.

Ever felt 'on the edge', desperately swinging from the very end of your rope? Maybe not in as extreme ways as Nikki or Julia – but I guess most of us have experienced edges of one kind or another and been tempted to let go, to fall in some way. Both story and poem remind me of Jesus' temptations in the desert, when he stood on two vertiginous physical edges. Also, after 40 days and nights without food he would have been at the dizzying end of his physical resources and on the edge of starvation doing irreparable damage to the tissues of his body. For these temptations to be real, he would also have needed to be on the edge of real danger of giving in to them. Here's his story. Read it carefully, with your own 'edges' in mind.

Then Jesus was led by the Spirit into the desert to be tempted by the devil. After fasting for forty days and forty nights, he was hungry. The tempter came to him and said, 'If you are the Son of God, tell these stones to become bread.'

Jesus answered, 'It is written: "Man does not live on bread alone, but on every word that comes from the mouth of God."'

Then the devil took him to the holy city and had him stand on the highest point of the temple. 'If you are the Son of God,' he said, 'throw yourself down. For it is written: "He will command his angels concerning you, and they will lift you up in their hands, so that you will not strike your foot against a stone."'

Jesus answered him, 'It is also written: "Do not put the Lord your God to the test."'

Again, the devil took him to a very high mountain and showed him all the kingdoms of the world and their splendour. 'All this I will give you,' he said, 'if you will bow down and worship me.'

Jesus said to him, 'Away from me, Satan! For it is written: "Worship the Lord your God, and serve him only."' Then the devil left him, and angels came and attended him.

When Jesus heard that John had been put in prison, he returned to Galilee. Leaving Nazareth, he went and lived in Capernaum.   (Matthew 4.1–13)

I included the last couple of verses because they show that, even after this extraordinary triumph at extreme edges, Jesus went back to face smaller, if still momentous edges – leaving home for the first time, starting his ministry, dangerous times, his cousin in prison . . . Great edges, little edges, we're not guaranteed an edge-free existence but we can trust that God will hold us – and, even if we should fall, that 'underneath are the everlasting arms' (Deuteronomy 33.27).

An impulse within some people pulls them to edges best avoided. The nature of those edges is different for each person. For example, I heard the other day about an alcoholic who had stayed 'dry' for years until someone sent her a box of liqueur chocolates. She tried one, started drinking again and before long her liver had given out . . .

If you know any spiritual or moral vertigo-sufferers, pray for them! Pray for any you know who find themselves on an extreme edge, perhaps of a physical, mental or relationship breakdown. And, however near or far we are from edges at present, let's pray for ourselves.

Lord, help us not to worry unduly about edges before we reach them. Prepare us in your own way and keep us close, so that when they loom at our feet, you can help us to hold on, trusting you to help us resist any forces which would pull us over. Amen.

Letting go of home and security

Dr Ronald Clements, a writer and researcher from Otford, Kent, writes:

> I cried when we left our home in Guildford. Not the manly thing to do, but I did cry. We weren't going far – I had a site job in Derbyshire. We weren't even selling our house, merely letting strangers occupy it – a tiny terraced cottage, two up, two down, built by the local brewery for its workers a century ago.
>
> More significantly it was our first home, the place where my wife and I had put our feet on the property ladder, established ourselves and had the first of our three daughters. There we had sat through the night, chipping stubborn plastic tiles from floorboards, devised a devious cat-flap system – unpatented – to confuse the neighbours' cats, grown vegetables at the bottom of the garden, decorated in our

own style, and applied the brightest yellow paint we could find to our front door.

We were away only 18 months – and six months later we sold that house. We were bound for China, believing this was God's plan for our future. The excitement of buying one-way tickets to live long-term alongside Asians meant we weren't so sad to leave that second time. Or perhaps we had discovered that we valued our special relationships with family and with God far more than our possessions or location. Those ties had been broken two years before when God gently eased our most costly purchase from our fingers.

From time to time we visit Guildford, making a small detour to drive past our first home. There is always something gratifying – 22 years later the house still has a very bright yellow front door.

By faith Abraham, when called to go to a place he would later receive as his inheritance, obeyed and went, even though he did not know where he was going. By faith he made his home in the promised land like a stranger in a foreign country; he lived in tents, as did Isaac and Jacob, who were heirs with him of the same promise. For he was looking forward to the city with foundations, whose architect and builder is God.   (Hebrews 11.8–10)

It's nice to settle, put down roots, have things sorted – and safe. Grow a garden with fruit and veg, build a strong house, cool in summer, warm in winter. Make friends. Nothing wrong with any of those things. But God always was a stirrer. And while our good is his concern, our comfort isn't always!

I thought I knew Abraham's story well. For example that he came from a town called Ur – always good for a laugh in Sunday school! Then suddenly God gave him instructions to move himself and his household to Canaan to become blessed as the father of a great nation. But I found that the impetus didn't begin in Ur. Genesis 11.31–32 says:

> Terah took his son Abram . . . and his daughter-in-law Sarai
> . . . together they set out from Ur of the Chaldeans to go to
> Canaan. But when they came to Haran, they settled there.
> Terah lived 205 years, and he died in Haran.

It seems that the 'letting go' – or perhaps the itchy feet – happened a whole generation earlier, and with no direct divine intervention. Or did God, in order to begin something new and important, start stirring things up – unsettling the whole family for years beforehand – as he did with the Clementses?

Abram's family set out for Canaan, yet settled in Haran, which was far enough from Ur to suffer the pain of letting go but only halfway to their goal. Why? The Bible is frustratingly concise sometimes! Genesis 12.4–5 says merely:

> So Abram left, as the LORD had told him; and Lot went with
> him. Abram was seventy-five years old when he set out
> from Haran. He took his wife Sarai, his nephew Lot, all the
> possessions they had accumulated and the people they had
> acquired in Haran, and they set out for the land of Canaan,
> and they arrived there.

Although the family left much behind in Ur, they accumulated more in Haran – people as well as possessions. 'And they arrived' in Canaan – that can't have been easy! They couldn't hop on a train or plane, nor hire removal lorries. Once there, they had nowhere to live but tents, for generations. Archaeologists study the remains of the great city that was Ur, whereas Canaan wasn't a city but an area. The family group would have moved around, striking camp, forever driving their sheep to new pastures. All we can know for sure is that Abram – and Sarai – had to let go of their old life and ways before they could hold on to an extraordinary promise, enter into a covenant relationship with God and, eventually, become Abraham, Sarah . . . and Isaac.

Carol Purves, a freelance writer from Carlisle, also felt insecure about relocation:

Although I'd travelled both at home and abroad, my roots were firmly in the south of England. All my schools, work, church, friends past and present had been below that famous Watford Gap, where I'd lived for every one of my 60-plus years – secure, safe and settled for life.

Sixteen months ago, with all my close family dead and distant relations in the north-east, I realized God was speaking to me. He wanted me to move – very specifically to Carlisle, a town I knew very slightly, where I had only one friend.

I argued with God. I was too old to make a fresh start. What about my church, friends, neighbours? How could I move physically with no family to help me? I didn't know enough about the area to choose a house. My own home had finally been decorated just as I wanted it. The north is cold and wet. God was asking me to give up too much.

I felt like Abraham, except I knew where God wanted me. The 360-mile distance seemed as far as any biblical journey. God had his way; I followed, afraid but trusting. With his help, I was able to let go.

God knows more about our lives than we do. I am now in the house he chose, worshipping in the church he chose. My health is better, I feel more alive – I merely existed before. Blessings are crowding in on every side but above all God is opening up new avenues of service for me. I don't know the full story yet, but I thank God that I was able to let go.

Lord, we love it when you comfort and reassure. But sometimes you unsettle and confuse us. Help us to realize that you're only helping us to let go of things which hold us – and your own plans – back. Help us in those times to hold tight to you and know that, even if the ride becomes so bumpy that we let go, you will keep holding on to us.

Pray for someone you know who is letting go of their old life and nervous about making a fresh start. Thank God that he makes fresh starts possible.

Letting go of security at work

Christine Barrett, a charity-shop manageress from Bournemouth, writes:

> Sometimes we need to let go of familiar and comfortable situations – and a career change certainly involves that.
>
> I worked in a doctors' surgery for many years and enjoyed what I did. I earned a reasonable salary, had a considerate boss, got on well with the other members of staff, but was becoming restless. Having done the job for years, I wondered if I was still giving it my best – and then there was the strong feeling that I'd love to be running a charity shop.
>
> I kept an eye on the local paper. Eventually it advertised a manager's position nice and close to home. But could I cope on the salary? The job felt right, so I applied – and was accepted, despite my lack of experience.
>
> I've been running the shop for seven years now, with a lovely team of volunteers and some really nice customers. We raise money for a good cause and we're environmentally friendly. My salary remains far from ideal, but I've learnt to manage on less.
>
> Now I've been approached about the possibility of running a charity shop for my church – a bit more money, but

less security. I would be opening a shop from scratch with no guarantee of success, and no head office or warehouse to support me. But if the project goes ahead and I'm offered the position, I'll take it – so long as I feel it's what God is asking me to do.

The last few years have taught me that the middle-class values of job security and status on which I was brought up are not necessarily the values of the kingdom of heaven.

Do not worry, saying, 'What shall we eat?' or 'What shall we drink?' or 'What shall we wear?' For the pagans run after all these things, and your heavenly Father knows that you need them. But seek first his kingdom and his righteousness, and all these things will be given to you as well. Therefore do not worry about tomorrow, for tomorrow will worry about itself. Each day has enough trouble of its own.

(Matthew 6.31–34)

A good job? Hang on to it.

Financial security and a pension? How wise!

Why would the family suffer? Most people work long hours these days.

There's more to life than nine to five? Or, more likely from 7.00 a.m. when you leave the house till 8.00 p.m. when you return? Grow up – a bit of hard graft never hurt anyone, especially if you want promotion. Protestant work ethic and all that.

You feel you'd like to do more to help others, or to understand a bit more about the world? Very noble I'm sure, but we can't all afford the luxury of dallying along that path, or where would our nation be?

Does any of that sound familiar, summing up the spirit of the age in which we live? What we eat, drink and wear have become so important that many of us 'run after' these things, working longer hours, causing ourselves more and more worry and stress.

There's a good deal in the Bible about perseverance, supporting one's family, even living rightly as a slave. But Jesus didn't say to anyone, 'Stick with your job.' He said, 'Follow me!' That involved his disciples letting go of their money, their security and all that was familiar and safe. It involved trusting him for their loved ones as well as themselves. It meant going on an adventure.

X Today Jesus still says, 'If you're holding on to me, my kingdom, my right way of living, you can let go of worry – leave that to me.' That's what faith means – and faith doesn't only concern 'religious' affairs but the very fabric of life. Jesus turns accepted norms upside down. His way, his 'righteousness' is seldom seen as the best way to live. That's because it involves letting go of so much that seems safe and good in order to hold on to someone we can't even see – who will take us we know not where.

Spend some time with the Lord, readjusting to his perspective. What kind of things do you worry about most? Where does your security lie? For whom are you most likely to take risks? Think – if we lived as radically as Jesus lived and taught, we would make even more of a difference.

Letting work go

Here we do not have an enduring city, but we are looking for the city that is to come.   (Hebrews 13.14)

Someone said, 'Constant change is here to stay.' That seems to be true, if not in heaven, then on earth. We are educated through a variety of means, then train for the workplace, only to find ourselves doing things at work for which we may have received no training or education at all. Later maybe we change tack because our employer goes bust or we're needed to look after family members, or have to stop work early for health reasons.

We may, or may not, enjoy our work. My brother aimed for retirement as soon as his career started, achieved it shortly after his fiftieth birthday and loves it. Nevertheless retirement, whether a person looks forward to it or not, might prove the biggest change of all. People find themselves lacking a structure for their time, missing status, colleagues, even technology – from photocopiers to computer experts. It's easy to feel lonely, useless, under the feet of other family members. Some find themselves with too many choices – and, at the same time, not enough. As people realize that they are growing old, health concerns add to money worries.

But constant change is what we can expect in this life and perhaps it's good to remind ourselves that all of it, including retirement, is a training or growing place for the 'city which is to come'. There work won't be tedious, we'll fulfil our potential, know and love our fellows better than we ever did and be together with one joyous aim, purpose and delight.

Meanwhile, here are two accounts of two very different people's retirement and how they coped with the changes. First, former working-all-hours engineer, Roger Madge, writes of letting his work go.

Have you ever overslept, woken up at 9.00 a.m. and had a panic attack – that you should already be somewhere else?

On 1 April 2006 that happened to me. I soon remembered that there was nothing to worry about because this was the first day of my retirement after about 40 years of going to work full-time.

The following days were like being on holiday. Then, in the quieter moments, came all sorts of nagging thoughts over things like my decision to quit, the amount of pension cover, ongoing health – and, over time, deeper questions about self-worth. In reality retiring is like changing jobs but I'd not done that for 30 years and this time had no manager to chase me – bliss, some would say!

A few years have passed since that April Fool's Day. I have worked through most of the changes and become involved with many new people and activities – all kinds of undreamt-of delights which are there to be enjoyed. An important part of coming to terms with my changing circumstances has been having a faith that is all about hope and new beginnings.

Ruth Bridger, who used to work for a research and advocacy charity as a project manager, writes:

My last day in full-time employment was memorable only for its complete lack of memorable events. The charity where I had worked for nearly five years had been taken over – some staff had already left, others were already working in a different location, leaving me alone, clearing up the legal paperwork, ensuring that assets were delivered to the correct recipients and leaving the rented office space as we had found it. I walked to reception, left my building access card and parking pass and stepped out into the late afternoon of a dull spring day. The weather matched my mood – an emptiness that I found difficult to face. No one to say goodbye to, no one to wish me a happy retirement, no farewell card or present . . . Even if I hadn't wanted to let go of full-time employment at age 56, it was certainly letting go of me.

I was also losing a good salary, the camaraderie of colleagues and the unpredictability of the 'media machine' which meant that I could be rushed off my feet from early in the morning to late at night, responding to radio and television demands as well as the national newspapers. This was what gave me a buzz, and I knew I would miss it. As my business cards dropped into the nearest wastepaper bin I also felt that I was letting go of my identity.

Now I was drifting off into uncharted waters; no anchor held me to the familiar. The wind was blowing my sails to unknown destinations, the shore was disappearing and the open sea beckoned. Of course, there was the obligatory list of things to do – get the garden into better shape, de-clutter the house, put all the photos into albums and read through the pile of books that exceeded the height of my bedside table. But what else?

In a short space of time, I had been offered a contract for approximately one day a week with a large charity, become company secretary of a new trading company set up by my church for the non-church activities within the building and found myself alongside a friend, who had no family and was facing surgery and months of treatment for cancer. Looking back, I had to let go, otherwise I could not have grasped all the new and surprising opportunities with both hands. Looking forward, I know that God, who is ever faithful and has been with me throughout all the changes of the past months and years, will continue to be with me.

Lord, help us all to hold things lightly, so that when a time of change comes we can let them go and grasp hold of new things which you are bringing our way. And if those new things mean a time of inactivity, of waiting, help us to use it to burrow deep into you, finding again our self-worth, even our companionship with you.

Letting go in generosity or with strings attached?

Each man should give what he has decided in his heart to give, not reluctantly or under compulsion, for God loves a cheerful giver. (2 Corinthians 9.7)

Give, and it will be given to you. A good measure, pressed down, shaken together and running over, will be poured into your lap. For with the measure you use, it will be measured to you. (Luke 6.38)

We love because he first loved us. (1 John 4.19)

Have you ever given, or received, a gift with strings attached? Not pleasant, is it? Leaves a strange taste in the mouth and may well damage relationships. I think it happens most often with gifts from parents to their children, but was astonished by an extreme example in a news item. A New York surgeon, who had generously given one of his own kidneys to save his wife's life, was now demanding it back. She had gone off with another man – and as part of the divorce settlement he asked his lawyers to argue for the return of his kidney, or a huge sum in compensation. I can understand that his actions stemmed from his sense of hurt and betrayal. But true giving surely involves letting go, for ever, no strings attached, no grasping back.

Jesus is so overwhelmingly generous. He took the initiative. The Father let him go to give everything for us before we even knew him – and when we betray him he keeps on giving and loving.

Anne Ripley wrote a piece with this theme, from her long-time experience of being a blood donor.

81

Blood – that rich red liquid that courses through our arteries and veins. It's ready for harvest every 16 weeks, so I have read.

Last time I went to give my 'pint' as usual, they told me that next time I would be due my gold card for 50 donations. They keep count. I don't bother.

I wonder sometimes how often my donation has contributed towards saving a life, but I shall never know. I hope I have saved a few. I am one of thousands, and we are all needed and more, to keep the stocks in the blood bank adequate.

There is one whose blood is unique. Jesus' blood is guaranteed – not to save life, but to save souls for eternal life – 100 per cent effective for 100 per cent of humanity. No incompatibility problems here. All anyone needs to do is to accept his gift, his donation.

And what a sacrifice! His life poured out in agony on the cross of shame. My donation is no sacrifice. Two cups of tea replace the fluid and in a few weeks my body has totally made up the blood cells lost.

Have you noticed God often works in that way? As we give, God gives back to us. So give – with a generous heart: money, time, skills, hospitality, even blood. God will repay.

Lord, give us generous hearts like yours, so that we let our gifts go freely, with no emotional or financial strings attached. If we're subsequently betrayed, as you were, help us to hold on, as you did, to love – and to yet more cheerful giving.

Letting go in creativity, worship, the emotions

My heart is stirred by a noble theme as I recite my verses for the king; my tongue is the pen of a skilful writer.

(Psalm 45.1)

Sorry, but it's me telling the story and . . . everything this time!

As a writer, I tend, in a spurt of inspiration, to 'let go'. I splurge everything on the page, then panic. Do I dare admit to imagining *that*? No way! (That's why I don't write much fiction. I'm much too uptight about my imaginings from thin air, thinking: who in their right mind would want to read them?) In non-fiction, I worry about being over-obvious and patronizing, inaccurate, waffly, obscure and irrelevant . . . Above all, how do I dare to write about God or interpret Scripture like that – anyway, the publisher will never accept it!

Anyone creative has to think about how their work will be received. The psalmist, whether speaking his verses to God or to an earthly king, would have been in awe of his audience too. Most writers will say that it's good to let go in creativity and then to ask those 'editing' questions, which are really all about whether your words are going to work for those who read or hear them. My first drafts improve hugely as I edit and even more as I cut. But I could go on editing and cutting until nothing was left – or until I'd lost all faith in my work. Eventually I have to say, 'Well, if it's no good my editor will say so.' That means trusting others with my work, including publishers' theological and other experts. If it weren't for their safety nets, I wouldn't be able to let go in creativity, or let my work go to be read at all because I'm not the best judge. When I've feared I've been far too wacky, my publishers have judged my writing fine.

It's not so different when we dare to let go in worship, whether silent or noisy. We need to trust that God will accept the extravagance of our heart and mind and soul and strength. 'O Lord, open my lips, and my mouth *will* declare your praise' (Psalm 51.15, my italics). Some of us need to let go of our fear, self-consciousness, feelings of unworthiness and all the rest. Instead of bottling them up, we could let our emotions go – as in this passage.

> When he came near the place where the road goes down the Mount of Olives, the whole crowd of disciples began joyfully to praise God in loud voices for all the miracles they had seen: 'Blessed is the king who comes in the name of the Lord!'
>
> 'Peace in heaven and glory in the highest!'
>
> Some of the Pharisees in the crowd said to Jesus, 'Teacher, rebuke your disciples!'
>
> 'I tell you,' he replied, 'if they keep quiet, the stones will cry out.' As he approached Jerusalem and saw the city, he wept over it. (Luke 19.37–41)

Your Creator has given you springs of creativity, a heart full of worship and a richness of emotion. Do you dare to 'let go' now, in your response to him?

Letting people go

Birth and death

'Do not let your hearts be troubled. Trust in God; trust also in me. In my Father's house are many rooms; if it were not so, I would have told you. I am going there to prepare a place for you . . . I will come back and take you to be with me that you also may be where I am. You know the way to the place where I am going.'

Thomas said to him, 'Lord, we don't know where you are going, so how can we know the way?'

Jesus answered, 'I am the way and the truth and the life. No-one comes to the Father except through me.'

(John 14.1–6)

Birth and death, both are hard to understand, especially when we've not experienced them before. They seem almost supernatural. So much is at stake (literally life or death!) yet we can't know exactly what will happen.

I'm told that, in the third stage of labour, mothers experience an almost irresistible urge to push their baby out. Not me: I held on. Pushing involves tension; tensing against the pain hurt, so I carried on relaxing, letting the pain of the contractions wash over me. I'd grown accustomed to the bulge underneath my maternity clothes where a new life kicked. I could keep that precious life safe inside me, but the journey down the birth canal is dangerous – and then the baby will have to breathe in the wide, cold world . . .

Of course, despite my reluctance to push him out, I knew what disasters would follow had I somehow held on and kept my firstborn in my womb. He's 28 now! I'd prepared a place for the baby, complete with cot, nappies, tiny clothes – all the paraphernalia, not to mention medical check-ups, books, advice . . . But when someone dies, we can only trust Jesus' words, his timing – and that he will go on caring for those of us remaining in this life too.

The disciples had it harder – having to let Jesus go away from them by a unique method, neither birth nor death. Knowing it was for a good purpose and that he would always be with them, he didn't seem upset about 'letting them go' – but at the time they were hard-pushed to understand either the purpose or the way.

Edwina Vardey, writer and editor, writes about the death of her artist husband.

He lay, eyes closed, in his bed from which he once could see his beloved garden. He was dying and had been slowly so doing for many years.

The district nurse had left the room and they, his wife and daughter, were watching alone. By the bed, propped up among the medicine bottles and glasses was a card with a prayer by Cardinal Newman. The daughter climbed on to the bed and whispered in her father's ear her love and admiration, talking to him of the journey he was about to take to a heaven full of all he loved – sunshine, bluebell woods, birdsong and his music played by long-dead friends. They waited.

The daughter felt that perhaps the word-painting of his worldly pleasures was holding him back. So they held his hands and silently prayed a version of Cardinal Newman's prayer.

Dear Lord, support him all the day long till the shades lengthen and the evening comes, and the busy world is hushed, and the fever of life is over, and his work is done. Then in your mercy give him a safe lodging, and a holy rest with peace at the last.

They waited.

Then his wife said, 'You were always the gentleman who let us go first – but this time you must show us the way.'

He smiled and died.

They opened the window and let in the birdsong and the smells of the spring garden and gave thanks.

Pray for those who watch at the bedside of dying loved ones. May they have a sense of when it is time to give them 'permission' to let go of this life and step forward into the place that Jesus went to prepare for them.

Children

We fetch your bottle, the metal pink one with the angel on it that you chose in Tesco's, and fill it with cool water from the kitchen tap. You are wearing your white T-shirt, the one we sewed with ribbons, tape and braid in random patterns – you held the thick needle in your small fingers. I am wishing you had chosen something more conventional but I keep my wish to myself.

We open the front door and walk out together up the slope of the drive. The sun is shining and you choose which way we go, then stop and pick a flower, a daisy from the grass verge. You push it into the buttonhole of my blue-grey cardigan.

You skip up the road on your strong legs, powerful, enjoying the movement. I liked skipping too. You notice a pink campion growing in the hedge and that also is picked and pushed into a buttonhole. I am breathing deeply, focusing on being smiley, being brave, acting like it's all OK, like all is well with the world – and in a way it is.

By the time we reach the end of Dowlans Road, my dowdy cardigan is adorned with a jumble of flowers, one in each hole. I can picture it now, the spray of white cow parsley, dainty Prussian-blue speedwell, the yellow dandelion, the red dead-nettle. You push a sprig of purple honesty into the last remaining hole and say, 'These are to love you when I'm gone.' I smile and thank you as tears seep from my eyes – I am grateful that you skip on and I wipe my face. I must be brave, must be strong.

We cross the road and meet up with Harry and Isabelle, your playschool friends, and the three of you run down the road. I chat with their mums, all of us trying to be smiley, brave and strong together.

In the playground I watch you scrambling up the grassy bank. I flash back to when I carried you in your baby sling and we took your brother for *his* first day at school. Memories of jam-tart-making, painting and snuggling on the sofa with books flicker through my mind's eye.

Then, 'Goodbye!' as Teacher guides you into the class-room. Those preschool days have finished. It's your turn now.

When early years consultant and mother Rachael Underwood tried to read her true story at my writing group she couldn't, she was in tears. As someone else read it for her, our hearts were in our mouths. Was her child dying? Even after the end of the story made it clear that her little girl was 'merely' starting school, most of our eyes were overflowing. Many were remembering that emotional day when we'd let our own children go into school for the first time – and the significance of that milestone in their gradual separation from us.

As a baby grows in the womb, and for quite a while afterwards, he or she depends on Mum 24/7 – exhausting but it does create strong bonds. We prepare our children for independence, knowing that things will have gone badly wrong if they need to remain womb-close for ever, yet we grieve the parting, the 'letting go' which must happen by slow degrees. Perhaps the most difficult time comes when they are still living with us, still of an age when, by law, we're responsible for them, though they may be taller than we are. Questions of how much to hold on or to let go really perplex us, then. Of course, whatever happens, in most cases a mother never lets go completely. She will always love her 'child'.

When I was expecting my second baby, the story of Hannah in the Bible struck me and we named our daughter partly for her. After the shame and persecution which barrenness had brought Hannah, God gave her a longed-for son.

> She named him Samuel, saying, 'Because I asked the LORD for him' . . .
>
> [Hannah] said to her husband, 'After the boy is weaned, I will take him and present him before the LORD, and he will live there always' . . .
>
> After he was weaned, she took the boy with her, young as he was . . . to the house of the LORD at Shiloh . . . She said to [the priest, Eli], '. . . I am the woman who stood here beside you praying to the LORD. I prayed for this child, and the LORD has granted me what I asked of him. So now I give him to the LORD. For his whole life . . .' (1 Samuel 1.20–28)

When Samuel was old enough not to need her breast milk any more, Hannah did not shirk from fulfilling her promise of letting him go to serve God at the temple. Given the kind of emotions we women experience, this is an extraordinary example of letting go! Yet I could so identify with the vivid detail as the story continued:

> Each year his mother made him a little robe and took it to him when she went up with her husband to offer the annual sacrifice. Eli would bless Elkanah and his wife, saying, 'May the LORD give you children by this woman to take the place of the one she prayed for and gave to the LORD.' Then they would go home. And the LORD was gracious to Hannah; she conceived and gave birth to three sons and two daughters. Meanwhile, the boy Samuel grew up in the presence of the LORD. (1 Samuel 2.19–21)

Hannah's surrender, her cheerful sacrifice, bore much fruit besides those children. Samuel went on to become a great prophet, helping save the nation – whereas Eli's own immoral sons might well have destroyed Israel's special relationship with God. They had to be let go, whereas through Samuel the Lord held everything together again.

If you have children, before you pray for them now, read this poem which Coral Kay wrote many years ago for her adopted daughter.

To my child
In the dark you grew,
Hidden from my view.
Then one day you came,
I called you by your name.
I looked on you and smiled
For you were now my child.
I kept you fed and warm,
Protected from all harm.

Then when you had grown
You learnt to stand alone.
Your life was in your hands
And I must loose the bands.
If you should walk away
There's nothing I can say.
But one thing you must know,
However far you go,
Whatever you may do
My love will go with you.

Wrong responsibility towards people

As Jesus and his disciples were on their way, he came to a village where a woman named Martha opened her home to him. She had a sister called Mary, who sat at the Lord's feet listening to what he said. But Martha was distracted by all the preparations that had to be made. She came to him and asked, 'Lord, don't you care that my sister has left me to do the work by myself? Tell her to help me!'

'Martha, Martha,' the Lord answered, 'you are worried and upset about many things, but only one thing is needed. Mary has chosen what is better.' (Luke 10.38–42)

It's so easy to latch on to the wrong things for which to be responsible. Those things may not be wrong in themselves. Jesus knew that meals have to be prepared – because to survive and function properly, people need food. How far would he and his disciples have got in their travels, had not women like Martha looked after that side of things? On the other hand when he fasted for 40 days and nights in the wilderness, he demonstrated that 'Man does not live on bread alone, but on every word that comes from the mouth of God' (Matthew 4.4). That means God's words are more important than food for our survival and well-being.

In that particular house in the village of Bethany, at that particular moment, they weren't fasting, yet Jesus knew that they all, including Martha, needed a different kind of food – one which doesn't require cooking. They needed to put everything else to one side and listen to Jesus' teaching. Martha's fussing distracted others besides herself. Her grumbles about the lack of help drew in Jesus, her sister Mary and more – imagine the tense atmosphere resulting from Martha's controlling behaviour.

Yet it was Martha's house – surely she had the right to feel responsible for the hospitality on offer? Yes . . . but what is the responsibility of a good hostess? Not to look good by producing the best meals in the neighbourhood. Jesus came to the heart of the matter when he said, 'Martha, Martha, you are worried and upset about many things, but only one thing is needed.' Driven by her anxiety, by the fact that she was so troubled, Martha's over-responsibility made her miss the one thing which none of them in the house could do without.

Luke says that it was Martha's house – not that of her brother Lazarus, nor of all three siblings. Was Lazarus a minor? Had their parents died? Did Martha, as the oldest sibling, take on responsibility for the family and their property? So much for young shoulders to bear – had she become too anxious to stop for a moment and listen even to this amazing man, who was to become the best friend the family would ever have? Once Jesus began teaching, did he lend Martha the grace and wisdom to let go of her nagging anxiety – and of the overbearing sense of responsibility which had caused it?

Deborah Jacob writes of how a sense of guilt drove her to take on wrong responsibility for her grown daughter – until Jesus intervened.

My older daughter Tanya and I once had a relationship that I would now call both volatile and co-dependent. Every time Tanya needed help I would jump to it, despite responsibilities for my other daughter Emily who still needed me, being 14 years younger than Tanya.

Like me, Tanya had her first child at around 19. Very soon she fell pregnant again – and her husband couldn't take the strain of two such little ones. He upped and left when her oldest was just two, and the youngest eight months. So I felt Tanya, at 21, needed me – she'd been through an extremely tough time. Plus her childhood wasn't the best as, among other things, I left her dad when she was only nine. I know now that I was guilt-driven, trying to make up for the emotional upheavals of her childhood.

For the next three years I ran around trying to make things better for her. Tanya would be OK with me one minute and blowing up the next. Because guilt drove me we would always end up with a massive argument. By now Tanya was 24, with three children under six. My youngest, Emily, was ten and used to get really fed up with the phone calls, so I felt torn between the two of them – and worn out.

Finally, I began to see that something had to change – Tanya had to learn to stand on her own two feet. I had to let go of her and her emotions – my own emotions too, especially the guilt. One day I was driving along, having just left Tanya, when I heard the words, 'It's time to cut the umbilical cord, to cut the apron strings.' I knew that was God. I'd never have seen it for myself! And, by then, I'd learnt to trust him. So I made a conscious decision and said out loud, 'OK, I cut the apron strings, I choose to cut the umbilical cord.'

I didn't just leave Tanya to it – the process took time, for both of us – but from that day all hell broke loose for about three years. Tanya worked through some huge issues. Because I had finally cut her loose to express herself fully, all of the past could come out, be dealt with and healed.

Her foundations had been on sand; 11 years on, they are on solid rock. She stands strong but, had I not let go when I did, she would not be the woman she is today. She not only stands on her own two feet, but is extremely wise and has raised three wonderful children, with whom she shares a lot of love. She shows empathy, understanding their needs far better than I ever understood hers as a child.

A huge learning curve through my life has been to see how, with the best of intentions, we can stunt the growth of another by stepping in and doing everything for them. No one person can supply what only God can give and we can rob others of the opportunity to look to him for strength to do things.

Ask the Holy Spirit if those things which you think of as your responsibilities come under the light yoke of his love and his grace. Or are you driven in them by strong negative forces such as guilt, pride or anxiety?

Loyalty

'Leave!' we said.

As the term progressed, all of us in my writing group had seen how Fiona was losing weight. She'd become haggard through sleeplessness and worry, a shadow of her normal creative and caring self. A line manager at work was bullying and taking every opportunity to undermine her, something which had never happened in all her career before, she said.

Letting people go

I can't imagine many would try bullying Fiona – she's not the type. 'You've an exceptional teaching track record over decades,' I told her. She'd taught disruptive teenagers inspiringly for years and now she'd tried everything at her disposal to resolve the problems at her current school – in vain. To me it was clear that she should find a different job, without worrying about letting the school or children down, since that school's management had failed to deal with the problems earlier, when she'd explained them.

Knowing how worried Fiona's husband and friends were, I concluded the time for mincing words had passed. 'Fiona, if you don't hand in your notice now you'll have a physical or nervous breakdown. That will do no one any good.'

Two years later, Fiona James wrote the story for this book:

Gone is my sense of guilt. Letting that job go caused me agony – mainly because I felt I was letting the students down. I'd stayed two terms. I'd never resigned without somewhere to go before but learnt the important lesson that I was not indispensable. My line manager tried to play that card, 'Who will teach them special needs now?'

'Well, you should have thought of that before you started shouting at me. Someone else will be able to do it,' I retorted.

'Leave me your lesson notes!' Panic rose in her voice.

'Fine, no problem.' The photocopier worked overtime, as I handed her the notes.

Now I have the courage to hand in my notice if necessary, without too many guilt pangs. I know that it is hard on the students but there are other teachers in the world. This term I have resigned from teaching some really violent students part-time in a very unsafe environment. While I attempted to cope alone, desperately hoping no one got injured, I kept trying to draw attention to these serious problems but the authorities took no notice. For me to have continued would have helped no one. Loyalty can be misguided and a burden.

Loyalty is good, isn't it? Something to hang on to. Yes, sometimes but, as in this passage or in Fiona's story, sometimes we need to let it go! We are not indispensable – and nor are leaders, Christian or otherwise, good or bad. Anyway, to whom should we be loyal? An experienced counsellor who read Fiona's story commented: 'Her loyalty has always been to the children, and each school tried to impose a second layer of institutional loyalty, at odds with her core values.' The same counsellor told me that she found the idea of letting go of loyalty interesting.

> When I'm working with families I find that loyalty can be of paramount importance because the collusion enables much to be hidden. Unquestioning loyalty can make people rigid, as they can no longer see other points of view.

Perhaps only Jesus deserves our unswerving loyalty. A number of years ago my husband and I sensed God was calling us to our present church after 20 years where we'd been nurtured and grown in another. Leaders from the first church said, 'But where is your commitment to us?'

My husband made a wise reply.

> Our commitment to you was never meant to last for ever, like a marriage vow. It's temporary, while we're part of this church. We're very grateful for the years we've spent with you but our overriding commitment is to Jesus – and to where he wants us to be.

Some people of course change their church, children's school, job, or partner almost as often as they change their clothes. As always, finding Jesus' wisdom on when to hold on and when to let go of loyalty to people is the key and we need to seek it in all humility.

> Since there is jealousy and quarrelling among you, are you not worldly? . . . When one says, 'I follow Paul,' and another, 'I follow Apollos,' are you not mere men? What, after all, is Apollos? And what is Paul? Only servants, through whom you came to believe – as the Lord has assigned to each his task. I planted the seed, Apollos watered it, but God made it grow . . . Whether Paul or Apollos or Cephas or the world or life or death or the present or the future – all are yours, and you are of Christ, and Christ is of God.
>
> (1 Corinthians 3.3–6, 22–23)

Lord, my motives are often so mixed, so tangled and confused. Help me to know your heart, ways and timing in this matter of loyalty to people, to commitments and to those I serve. Help me hold on to my loyalty to you.

Holding on to duty – and everyone's burdens

> Carry each other's burdens, and in this way you will fulfil the law of Christ. If anyone thinks he is something when he is nothing, he deceives himself. Each one should test his own actions. Then he can take pride in himself, without comparing himself to somebody else, for each one should carry his own load.
> (Galatians 6.2–5)

> Come to me, all you who are weary and burdened, and I will give you rest. Take my yoke upon you and learn from me, for I am gentle and humble in heart, and you will find rest for your souls. For my yoke is easy and my burden is light.
> (Matthew 11.28–30)

Carry each other's burdens, carry your own load, carry Jesus' yoke. Even though the latter is said to be 'light' all this seems far too much. I confess to feeling weighed down, even complaining sometimes of the unreasonably heavy load that Christians have to carry. We hear of terrible disasters around the world and feel we have to respond. We must help our neighbours – all of them – and serve our church too, while putting our families (no, Jesus!) first. We're meant to set the oppressed free in his name, pray without ceasing, be 'salt and light', support our own communities while giving practical and financial help to all kinds of causes. Easy? Light? I'm exhausted and guilt-ridden merely typing the doubtless incomplete list! Surely we don't have to hold on to all this weight but can let it go sometimes?

Recently I was talking with a psychiatrist about my concerns for a woman who suffers recurrent bouts of clinical depression. 'If only she would stop trying to save the world!' the psychiatrist said. 'If she hears of anyone in need of help, she thinks she's responsible, takes on the whole thing alone, does the same again and again with other people's problems and finally collapses.'

I once ghostwrote a book for Roger Altman who co-founded the Association of Christian Counsellors. He and his wife would listen to people's pain – terrible things, day after day. I asked how they coped without being dragged down themselves. 'If at the end of the day I can't leave all that on my desk, go out and enjoy the sunset, or a good laugh over a meal with the family,' Roger said, 'I know that it's time to stop.' Anyone in that line of service has to learn how to let go, remain detached and set boundaries. Otherwise they will either go under themselves or become the kind of do-gooders who damage those they are trying to help. As

C. S. Lewis wrote in *The Screwtape Letters*: 'She lives for others; you can recognize the others by their hunted look.'

We need to bear others' burdens, of course we do – and at another time different people might lighten ours. We also need to lean on Jesus, letting him bear our burdens – after all, he suffered on the cross partly in order to do that. Sometimes circumstances become so extreme that we need to let go – and allow other people, alongside Jesus, to hold *all* of our burdens.

Julia Nelson, would-be novelist, writes some good sense about a 'milder' case:

My best friend Charlotte had a terrible childhood. With both parents alcoholics, she was very neglected and she had found happiness only when she met her partner of 20 years. Nonetheless, to me, her childhood experience still informs everything in her life. On many levels this has proved positive. Charlotte saw herself through grammar school, won a scholarship, and went on to become a highly motivated and successful senior executive at a big multinational company – one of only four women worldwide to reach her level of seniority there. Effusively generous with her time – towards friends, the local church, anyone that asks her – she gives profusely to charities, particularly those in aid of children and animals. She is extremely sentimental, especially when under the influence, a parental trait she did not manage to shun completely.

I can't help feeling that, following an awful childhood, Charlotte is now on a one-woman crusade to right all the ills of the world – or at least those in her general vicinity. A good example is this: she and her long-term partner are about to marry. She has two daughters – one is my eldest daughter's best friend. She promised both my girls that they could be bridesmaids, then stopped and thought – but all my daughter's other friends will not feel valued if I don't ask them too. Since her daughter has many friends, it was entirely possible Charlotte would have more bridesmaids than Lady Diana. In the end I told her she should feel under no obligation to anyone's child, including, reluctantly, my own – I knew that her partner has only limited tolerance of other people's children. Shouldn't she abandon her warped sense of duty and stick with her own daughters as bridesmaids?

Her mother died, without very much outward lamentation on her part, a few years ago, and her father is dead too. She is about to marry her university sweetheart. Although her childhood experience has made her a very generous and thoughtful person, Charlotte also expends a lot of time and stress on maintaining this 'Mother Teresa' ethos. Now I hope that she can let the past go and enjoy life a little more for herself.

Lord, it's never easy to know when to hold on to a burden and when to let it go, especially if the burden belongs to someone else. We know you call us to love beyond where it hurts but we need your grace so that we're not driven by duty or by the need which we perceive in others. Only you are the Saviour of the world. Carry us on the wide river of your amazing love, which will support and refresh us as we help those whom you want us to help. Amen.

Am I my family's keeper? When is it time to let go?

Then the LORD said to Cain, 'Where is your brother Abel?' 'I don't know,' he replied. 'Am I my brother's keeper?'

(Genesis 4.9)

When am I my mother's, father's, brother's, sister's or grown children's keeper? Or when would it be better for all concerned to let someone else take responsibility? I'm thinking mainly of when a person cannot take much responsibility for himself or herself. Clearly, we're all responsible not to murder our relatives, as Cain had killed his brother, Abel, and then tried to claim innocence and ignorance. But what if caring for one family member makes life so impossible that the rest of the family's sanity, or very existence together, is threatened? What if the person causing all the bother is our mother or father? If their behaviour is becoming increasingly unreasonable and obstinate, or over-dependent, perhaps because of dementia, pain, or fear? Age can exaggerate all the worst aspects of someone's personality.

We're told to honour our father and mother – and that includes looking after them in old age. Is it honouring to 'put them in a home'? If so, at what point? I've seen so many middle-aged people agonizing over how much longer they are going to be able to hold on, keeping the generations together, dealing with crisis after crisis. They can feel like the rope in a tug of war, with the people they love and care for each pulling them in different directions. Tensions rise, emotions boil over, tempers snap, guilt closes in like a thundercloud. Eventually something or someone has to give, to let go – one hopes as gently as possible!

Perhaps the whole situation has been made worse by years of shared history (and histrionics?). Perhaps family members involved are too similar, sharing weak points, or those responsible for caring no longer have the physical or mental strength. Perhaps it is time to let go.

When I first met Sue Wall she had a demanding job as the bursar of a large school, many miles from where she lived. Sue is a very caring Christian. Though I knew she'd had problems with her mother, I never realized their extent, until she wrote me this piece entitled: 'Letting Mother Go'.

Could I have coped any longer? I am not sure. I certainly felt at breaking point. For 33 years my mother had been part of our household. Never one to cook or keep house, on the untimely death of my father she was lost. Mum had never even written a cheque! The only thing for everyone's sanity was to all live together.

There followed a frenetic few months: two houses were sold and a larger one purchased and converted for the needs of three generations. Mother was now just 62, and our children three-and-a-half and five. We may as well have had three children! My mum didn't need a kitchen, she didn't cook. Her social life resembled a teenager's – if we wanted to go out we had to find a babysitter, she was never available. She had a male escort always but never remarried – not for the lack of being asked. She'd declare that if my father wasn't there to see to her needs, then I was the next best thing.

As my children grew older they would often 'babysit' Granny, should she have nothing planned for the evening. She hated her own company and would not stay alone.

In her late eighties she started to become frail, although still very capable of playing a fair hand of whist and doing the odd sequence dance. She needed help to bathe and dress, still allowing only me to do it and flatly refusing a carer while I worked. Her ability to use the telephone never left her and she would phone me at work, often several times an hour. My staff were wonderful and talked her round from many a difficult situation – often without troubling me.

I knew the time was coming to let her go and allow someone else to assume her care. Her needs were too complex; several times each night she needed attention. Dawn, with all its own routines, always followed a bad night.

It's a monumentally difficult decision, which only the main carer can make and I will never, never forget the day I let her go, or did I abandon her? That's how she saw it. The home was nice, she had a lovely en-suite room – but hated everything about it. She'd still telephone morning, noon and night, even making the nurses ask if I thought they were doing the right thing! I always said, 'Yes.'

I had let Mother go!

Pray for someone you know who is in a difficult caring role. Is there anything you can do to give some respite? Pray for those feeling guilty for not being able to care 'enough', that they might let false guilt go, along with the weight of unbearable responsibility.

Letting go – and holding on – in old age

Though no spring chicken herself, Sylvena's understanding of and love for the elderly shines out of her. Left alone after a decade of bereavements, including the sadness of seeing her elderly father misunderstood at times when he needed care, she didn't mope. Instead she threw herself into helping older people understand that they are still valued and that there is hope. When I met her she was working for the London City Mission in a London care home, using all kinds of creative ideas and investing immense amounts of time, energy and love. She told me:

People entering residential care often feel that they've lost everything: independence; their own home, church and possessions; health, hearing, sight, mobility or even their memories and their mind. Friends and perhaps spouse will have died . . . Letting go is so painful and often people feel abandoned – but Jesus is there for them, caring for them – that's what I want to show. There's always something for them to hold on to, for example they can still give and receive joy and love.

Sylvena explained how one old woman emerged from her slough of despond when encouraged to make a brightly coloured 'butterfly' by a simple marbling technique.

'Did I make that?' the elderly woman exclaimed in delight. 'I thought my days for such wonders long over!'

'You know, you can be a butterfly.' Sylvena shared Jesus' message of new life with that elderly woman. She didn't come to faith, but seeing her involved in life again was like watching a butterfly emerge from its chrysalis there and then.

Sylvena Farrant wrote the following poem out of her experience of working with the elderly.

> **Hold on – let go, let God!**
> I'm frightened, Lord, to let go and yet I'm having to – fast!
> Will my hold on you be strong enough to last?
> Independence is becoming dependence – on you or who?
> I'm frightened, Lord, to let go, but what am I going to do?
> What will happen if my mind goes?
> Will I be aware of you then?
> Or be at the mercy of men?
> Keep me close, Lord, in all the ups and downs of this life.
> Nothing has prepared me for such savage changes in old age,
> Loss of sight, sound and smell – a prisoner in a rotting cage.
>
> But thinking of it, Lord – what do I panic for?
> You have promised never to leave or forsake me,
> Whatever the future may have in store.
> So it's not my hold on you that counts
> But your hold on me – *that* is forever sure!

> Thank you, Lord for love such as this
> Help me not to fret or worry –
> And so your perfect peace to miss –
> But look to you and love you more and more.

Whatever our age, we do need to 'let go' of some things, or at least hold them lightly, while we are held by certain truths which help dispel fear of the ultimate 'letting go' in death. Can you identify those holdings on and lettings go in the following Bible passage?

> I write to you, fathers, because you have known him who is from the beginning. I write to you, young men, because you have overcome the evil one. I write to you, dear children, because you have known the Father. I write to you, fathers, because you have known him who is from the beginning. I write to you, young men, because you are strong, and the word of God lives in you, and you have overcome the evil one. Do not love the world or anything in the world. If anyone loves the world, the love of the Father is not in him. For everything in the world – the cravings of sinful man, the lust of his eyes and the boasting of what he has and does – comes not from the Father but from the world. The world and its desires pass away, but the man who does the will of God lives for ever.   (1 John 2.13–17)

In St John's time, the older members of society were respected – whereas today they are often 'let go', in the sense of being forgotten. Meditate on the Bible passage – and perhaps use Sylvena's poem, and this one on the next page by retired teacher Sylvia Herbert, to increase your compassion for the elderly who may need our help to hold on.

Spending Time

I led you gently to a garden chair,
You had a book, a shady hat to wear,
A glass of sparkling wine to show I care,
Bright flowers round about you, everywhere.

Inside, I hurried to complete my chores.
Intent, I laboured on without a pause,
Until, by chance, I cast a glance outdoors
And saw you, dreaming of those distant shores

To which age bears you, far away from here;
Already, in your eyes a hint of fear.
I ran out, clasped your hand and held you near.
You said, 'I'm lonely by myself, my dear.'

In death

The LORD said to Moses, 'Now the day of your death is near. Call Joshua . . . I will commission him' . . .

'Now write down . . . this song and teach it to the Israelites and make them sing it . . . I know what they are disposed to do, even before I bring them into the land I promised them on oath.'

So Moses wrote down this song that day and taught it to the Israelites . . . [and] finished writing in a book the words of this law from beginning to end . . . 'Take to heart all the words . . . so that you may command your children to obey carefully . . . By them you will live long in the land you are crossing the Jordan to possess.'

On that same day the LORD told Moses, 'Go up . . . to Mount Nebo in Moab . . . and view Canaan, the land I am giving the Israelites as their own possession. There on the mountain that you have climbed you will die and be gathered to your people . . . because . . . you broke faith with me in the presence of the Israelites . . . you will see the land only from a distance.'

This is the blessing that Moses the man of God pronounced on the Israelites before his death . . .

Moses was a hundred and twenty years old when he died, yet his eyes were not weak nor his strength gone . . . Now Joshua son of Nun was filled with the spirit of wisdom because Moses had laid his hands on him.

(Deuteronomy 31.14—34.9)

That is a long and unusual account of the ultimate letting go – a person's death. You might like to take some time to read the whole Bible story which I've abridged above. We know that, despite his earlier sin, Moses 'rested with his fathers' after his death and that he appeared on another mountain at Jesus' transfiguration. I don't suppose God tells many of us exactly when and where we are going to die and few are given detailed, specific instructions such as Moses received to prepare for his death. Of course his instructions, including song-writing and mountain-climbing, were necessary for the sake of the nation which he led. It's also true that, 'no prophet has risen in Israel like Moses, whom the LORD knew face to face' (Deuteronomy 34.10). But since we in the new covenant also know God face to face, maybe we should be asking him to make clear any preparations we need to make for death.

Talking of guidance, for a couple of days I'd been asking God to show me a theme for this new book and, as I half-woke early that Sunday morning two clear words broke through my contented sleepiness while I was still in bed – 'letting go'. About an hour later my ears pricked up in church. Mel Commandeur, one of our ministers, was speaking. Before training for the ministry, Mel was a nurse and had spoken before about the special grace she often saw at work in hospital around the time of patients' deaths. Now she was saying how much better if the terminally ill let go and prepare for a good death rather than spending all their energy in fighting for another few days of life. After the service I asked if she'd write a specific story about this for my new book – and here it is.

I didn't know Steve in the peak of his health, at the zenith of his career or the heights of his brilliance. I never knew him at the top of the world, but I met him in his finest hour. I'd never seen him healthy, so didn't realize how ill he was. Neither of us knew at the moment of our introduction that he had 33 days left to live – he told me that he might be dying, but we both imagined months rather than days. His will and world told him that cancer is there to be fought, not negotiated with. Death is evil, not something to be considered and certainly not to be embraced. But had you tried the path of brave resistance and allowed the chemo needle to toxify every vein and avenue of your being, had you stood tottering in the wake of its onslaught and still it wouldn't blink, then perhaps you'd see forgiveness for the one who thinks: 'I've had enough, perhaps there is another way . . .'

What if the other way is waiting and not fighting, seeking instead of trying to outstare the enemy? The way of letting go needs permission – from loved ones, friends, the medical profession and the media. It might not be forthcoming because of the mantra: 'Cancer is there to be fought: everyone affected has a duty to beat it or go down trying.' Where is the permission to think, reflect on life and prepare to die well? Who will say it's OK to celebrate all that has been good, all that is a gift – and then let go? How do you ask for permission to help those around you to accept your exit when they want you to fight on? They accuse you of giving up hope if you talk about death, so how can you explore the hope that lies beyond the door of death?

My friend Steve used his 33 days with infinite wisdom: he made practical arrangements, had conversations with family, business partners and friends. You could say he'd given up hope, but he was saying aloud his hopes for others' future, for his wife and his beautiful little girls. This was never the business of a hopeless man. He asked for a priest to walk with him down the lonely corridors of questions, shame, doubt and fear – dark corridors, but death became his door, not the end to hope.

My friend Steve showed me how to shift the focus from clinging to life at all costs to dying with dignity. He was quietly joyful, unafraid and at peace. This is dying well, and it comes not to those who fight, but to those who find the courage to listen and to wait.

Lord, old hymns often end with a prayer that you'll be with us at the time of our death and I've tended to dismiss that as 'Victorian obsession'. But now I pray that you will show me, at the right time, what I need to do in preparation for my death, especially to prepare those I love.

Help us all to pray for those with a terminal diagnosis – and those whom they love – that both will be allowed to let go, and hold on, to those things which you require of them. Amen.

Laying down your life

Greater love has no-one than this, that he lay down his life
for his friends.   (John 15.13)

I don't feel I have any right at all to comment on this. To do so would be glib, so instead here are two stories and a poem.

Jack's story

My father-in-law, Jack Leonard, had a terrible war in the Far East. Born in 1916, he was called up in 1940 and trained as a gunner in Wales. They sent him to Singapore where, after two days, his company was deployed to Kota Baharu on the western side of the northern Malay peninsular, up near the Thai border and eight miles from the North China Sea. There he undertook five months more gun training before the Japanese landed in December 1941. Though the Allies had a large modern airbase at Kota Baharu they lacked the planes to give air cover. In the first and one of the most violent battles of the Pacific campaign, their system of defensive beach bunkers gave way and the British received permission to withdraw.

The Japanese captured the town on 9 December and took over the airbase which gave them air, sea and land control of the area. It must have been somewhere in the midst of these fast-moving events that Jack answered the call to stay behind for a rearguard action, while the rest of his company was evacuated by ship. The few volunteers required would face almost certain death. Jack volunteered. They did what they could, then escaped south, walking almost 300 miles as the crow flies, down through the jungles of Malaya, avoiding snakes and Japanese snipers until they reached Singapore. There they learnt that the ship which had evacuated the others had been torpedoed, with all lives lost.

So, Jack, with no wife or children at that time, had been willing to lose his life and had saved it, while those who understandably chose to save their lives had lost them. It wasn't quite that straightforward, though. Jack said that when the small group of surviving rearguarders arrived in

Singapore in late January, they didn't realize that the Allies there were about to surrender. Jack said, 'It was a right shambles.' Within a few days he and the other 'volunteers' found themselves escorting sailors from other ships, through straits defended by the Japanese, on a Dutch ship which wasn't even fitted out for war. All the ships were hit but, remarkably, Jack's life was spared yet again. He'd run out of bullets for his machine gun, saw a chap staggering towards him with a fresh belt of them and ran over to him, just as a Japanese rocket hit his gun.

They survived, reaching Java shortly before the Japanese landed there too – and Jack walked the island's whole width to escape. Jack told us that someone made a feature film about that episode later. He lived to fight on the Indian sub-continent and, worst of all, in the Burma campaign. He would never talk about that. When he was 86 and dying it became clear that he had never lost his faith but ever since the war he had refused to join in God-talk or to have anything to do with church – and he never wanted to travel outside of Britain again. He was a good man; he married and had a son whom I married. Our family wouldn't be here without Jack. Of course we thank God that though he was willing to let his life go in the service of his country, remarkably he was protected all through those dangerous war years. We recognize that his experiences weren't without ongoing cost to him, though.

Eric's story

In 1943, when just 18 and freshly trained as a radio operator, Eric Leat was on a troopship, part of a convoy from Greenock, heading for the Far East via South Africa. Because of spies in Ireland, their route lay far out in the

Atlantic, where German U-boats attacked. As the convoy was being torpedoed, a Welsh regiment on Eric's ship struck up with the hymn, 'Guide me, O thou great Jehovah'. Eric wrote:

> Then we heard across the waters the next ship singing, 'Strong deliverer, be thou still my strength and shield.' The great words, the thrilling tune, were taken up from one ship to another throughout the convoy.
>
> Long after the war, when my navy days were no more than a distant memory, I told this story and a man in the group said, 'I was there. I was in the Merchant Navy on one of the troopships. Yes, an unforgettable experience, everybody suddenly burst out singing.'

Escort ships would try to pick up survivors from stricken vessels but troopships under attack were not allowed to stop, so Eric could never find out how many survived, nor even how many ships sank in that attack, though they thought they counted three. He thanks God for deliverance as he remembers the singing, but also thinks of those who were lost – and what it must have been like for them, desperately clinging on to life in that cold ocean. In 2008 he wrote a poem which he gave to me, 'For your book on letting go,' he said. 'And holding on.'

> **Musical chairs – 1943**
> There was never room enough
> For everyone in the boats
> Women and children of course;
> We were supposed to be men,
> Eighteen years old, our first ship.
> The cold, cold Atlantic.

Kept afloat by a lifebelt,
Drifting in and out of sleep,
In and out of prayers.
Back in my childhood again
Playing musical chairs;
Never enough room for all,
Someone left out in the cold.

The pretty girl with dark eyes:
I gave up my seat to her
And she went on to win
And to forget about me.
Remember her soft brown hair;
Out in the cold Atlantic
Never enough chairs
When the music stops.

The sick bay we called Rose Cottage
No one knows why. And I
Don't know how I was rescued
Nor how fit I shall be
To play the games again –
Those games of war and waves
And musical chairs.

Pray for those who were – and are – willing literally to lay down (or let go of) their lives for their friends, or for the freedom of future generations. Pray for those who survive but are damaged, physically or psychologically.

Essentials

Tensions and paradoxes

> Every year his parents went to Jerusalem for the Feast of the
> Passover. When he was twelve years old . . . After the Feast
> was over, while his parents were returning home, the boy
> Jesus stayed behind in Jerusalem, but they were unaware of
> it. Thinking he was in their company, they travelled on for
> a day. Then they began looking for him among their rela-
> tives and friends. When they did not find him, they went back
> to Jerusalem to look for him. After three days they found him
> in the temple courts, sitting among the teachers, listening to
> them and asking them questions.   (Luke 2.41–46)

Nine days' journey from Nazareth to Jerusalem, on foot or
by donkey, and nine days back – for the young people it's
an annual holiday, with nearly the whole village travelling
down together for the Passover every year.

Jesus is twelve now – newly grown-up! Mary and Joseph
have his younger brothers to look after as they set off back
to Nazareth. Jesus is a good lad, knows the way and will be
safe and happy with the other young people – let him go
with them. But as they reach their resting place at the end
of the first day's journey, Jesus is nowhere to be found.
It's every parent's nightmare – and this couple have been
charged with the care of a very special young person indeed.

Parents of growing children soon find out about tensions and paradoxes – how far to hold on and when to let

115

their offspring go. The right course of action is by no means obvious. Mary and Joseph don't understand when Jesus, once found, replies to their worried remonstrance, 'Why were you searching for me? . . . Didn't you know that I had to be in my Father's house?'

They have to learn from their son what is right; it takes time, even when their son is Jesus. Maybe the best way all can learn as parents *is* from Jesus. How we need 'wisdom from above'! (James 3.17, Good News Bible). Take children with profound autism. In what freedom of choice, what opportunities can you encourage them? What risks and pleasures make their life worth living? How can parents create opportunities to give and receive love – when the condition militates against that? Holding on as well as letting go takes huge love and creative effort – helped by seeing the person's value through God's as well as human eyes.

Morag Bramwell from Scotland's Black Isle wrote this poem to accompany a photo exhibited as part of the Highland Carers Project and Princess Royal Trust for Carers. It shows her friend, musician Isabel Paterson, playing the piano with her autistic son Matthew sitting on her knee. They titled the poem 'Friday's child' – according to the nursery rhyme he is 'loving and giving'. It expresses so well the transforming paradox when God's and human grace combine.

> Behold my son
> With whom I am well pleased.
> I care with a Passion
> As you care for me
> I feel for this, my son,
> Your gift,

With words of music
Heaven sent
I'll be your Instrument.

Even in more 'normal' circumstances, you never know what may be around the corner. Ruth Cunningham writes movingly of an occasion when, having largely let a grown child go to lead his own life, they needed to hold on again – and of the tensions and paradoxes when she and her husband could begin to let go again, little by little.

To hold on – or to let go? Is it possible to do both at the same time? My answer, I think, would be 'yes'.

We'd watched our son grow up from a clingy baby and toddler, through excitement-filled childhood, rebellious teenage years, until the time came for letting go as he moved to live and work in London.

The years passed – occasional visits – occasional phone calls. His career progressed – new duties, new responsibilities, new demands – longer and longer hours. Until that dreadful day . . .

A faltering voice – 'Mrs Cunningham – I'm sorry but David has been missing for eight days.'

We never hear about the prodigal son's mother. I know how she felt – but there are no words to describe it – maybe that's why we never hear about her. Now I know what people mean when they say they feel as though they've been punched in the stomach. The next week was a blur – sleep eluded us, everything else was forgotten, nothing else mattered. Until that amazing day . . .

A faltering voice – 'Mum, it's me.'

All the questions we might have had evaporated – they simply didn't matter. He was safe. He was alive.

Since that day we have tried together to make sense of it all and fill in the gaps of just what happened in those two interminable weeks after what had clearly been some kind of breakdown. It has never really been resolved, but maybe that's no bad thing – maybe that would just be too painful.

Recovery has been slow. Even after all this time, the healing process continues – but it is happening. We haven't wanted to let go again – the prospect terrifies – and yet we know that we must. We must allow him again to have the confidence to move on in a different, as yet unknown, direction. But in that 'letting go' we know that there will always be a 'holding on'. An invisible thread – invisible, but strong – it must be. Visits and phone calls are more frequent, emotional demands gradually diminishing and something close to normality seems to be within reach.

So – to return to my question – can we hold on and let go at the same time? I can only answer with another question – can we possibly do otherwise?

Jesus, you were a living paradox – God and human being, mortal and immortal, Lord of all and child who, after teaching learned men, returned to obey your parents. You hold humankind and even the universe in a creative tension. At the same time you let us go with our free will and hold on – sustaining and transforming what we destroy. We can't begin to understand but we worship you and implore your wisdom as we face difficult decisions. We pray particularly for parents whose children are not obedient, who have special needs or whose health breaks down so they need 'holding' far beyond the norm. Give wisdom about maintaining boundaries, and about which risks to take. Amen.

Letting go of the good and receiving the best

As he looked up, Jesus saw the rich putting their gifts into the temple treasury. He also saw a poor widow put in two very small copper coins. 'I tell you the truth,' he said, 'this poor widow has put in more than all the others. All these people gave their gifts out of their wealth; but she out of her poverty put in all she had to live on.'

Some of his disciples were remarking about how the temple was adorned with beautiful stones and with gifts dedicated to God. But Jesus said, 'As for what you see here, the time will come when not one stone will be left on another; every one of them will be thrown down.'

(Luke 21.1–6)

If God owns the universe, clearly he doesn't need our gifts but he does want us to become more like him – generous and full of grace, holding material things lightly, rather than letting them weigh or even tie us down. I could look after my house much more easily if I took that advice! As for the widow, giving away all she had to live on meant that she had to trust God completely. She could have complained that, according to the law, the temple authorities should have been giving her alms. She could have tried to kick up a fuss in order to hold on to her rights. Instead she showed the religious leaders Jesus' radical new way, as she threw herself on God's mercy.

Jesus went on to say that the whole system, which had become so corrupt, so out of tune with God and his heart for the poor, would be destroyed and a time of chaos and persecution would ensue. Exactly that happened when Jerusalem fell in AD 70. The disciples would be caught up in it but Jesus told them: 'By standing firm you will gain life' (Luke 21.19). The widow too, surely, would gain life, eternal life, through Jesus' sacrifice and her own demonstrable faith. No money, no human gift can buy something so precious.

Giving is but one incidence of holding things lightly – of showing trust in God by being prepared to let go of what is good. Exercising our small faith through giving perhaps helps us to receive his great wells of grace which help us through. After letting go of something good which you value highly, how often have you received the best in its place?

Kathleen Gillum, a widow from Teddington in Middlesex, writes:

I had lived in my home for over 20 years. My husband and I had converted it into a pretty cottage with oak-beamed ceilings and lattice windowpanes. Roses and honeysuckle grew around the door and wisteria climbed all over the porch.

I loved my little house and it had become my sanctuary, especially after my husband had died. I had never intended leaving it. Then I was diagnosed with a heart problem. Knowing that the huge garden had become too difficult to manage I kept toying with the idea of moving – but how could I ever leave my secure haven?

It had three bedrooms whereas my son and his family had a two-bedroomed flat. Now there was an idea! Perhaps we could swap living accommodation? I prayed, asking the Lord to help me in making a decision. Finally I concluded that it was right to swap. I knew that my son and his family, especially the two children, would love the freedom of the garden and a bigger place to live but I was still worried, expecting tears and second thoughts. 'Please, Lord, don't let me be too sentimental about hanging on to my house!'

When moving day arrived, an amazing sense of peace enveloped me and I felt totally calm. Now I have a beautiful, spacious flat. The sun streams into the rooms. A gorgeous cherry tree outside my window blossomed this spring and looked so wonderful with its white flowers that I call it 'my snowflake tree'.

What I had felt would be a sacrificial act turned out a real blessing to all of us. Amazingly, since then the hospital told me I have no heart problem. I am so glad I trusted God to help me let go and move forward to a brand new start, with no dread, no tears and no regrets.

Lord, when it comes to times when you seem to be asking us to let go of the good, familiar things we trust, give us the grace to fall backwards, knowing, even when we can't see, that you are there to catch us and hold us secure in your embrace.

Keeping on holding on

I waited patiently for the LORD; he turned to me and heard my cry. He lifted me out of the slimy pit, out of the mud and mire; he set my feet on a rock and gave me a firm place to stand . . .

Do not withhold your mercy from me, O LORD; may your love and your truth always protect me. For troubles without number surround me; my sins have overtaken me, and I cannot see. They are more than the hairs of my head, and my heart fails within me. Be pleased, O LORD, to save me; O LORD, come quickly to help me . . .

I am poor and needy; may the Lord think of me. You are my help and my deliverer; O my God, do not delay.

(Psalm 40.1–2, 11–13, 17)

Interesting psalm, this – there's a dramatic rescue. Then danger and need lead again to more desperate cries. That's hard. It's hard to hold on when God rescues you from one crisis – but then, because the situation is ongoing, the pressure builds again. Can you keep asking him for help? Yes. Isn't that a sign of failure? No.

I was leading a writing holiday at the wonderful Christian conference centre of Lee Abbey, on the Exmoor coast of north Devon. In that part of the country there's hardly an inch of flat ground. Cliffs plunge to the sea, valleys are steep and narrow, hills high. On the approach to Lee Abbey, in the unique 'Valley of Rocks', only a herd of wild goats are at home scampering over its rocky crags, its boulders and its precipitous scree.

On the first complete day of the writing holiday, multi-talented artist and now carer Anne Beer sat down, alone and mentally exhausted, in the Valley of Rocks. Here she continues the story in her own words:

> With my personal life being under much pressure, I sat down to contemplate my situation. How easy it would be to end it all by jumping off the edge and into the depths of the sea.
>
> As I painted the scene before me, I came to realize that I felt as though I had been stuck on the slippery scree between the highest and the lowest rocks. I made the decision to choose the highest rock of all and put my feet back on that Rock – and never to wander from that path again. It felt so good. Thank you, Lord.

After that the whole group had the joy of seeing an extraordinary transformation in Anne. The following day she shared with us a little of what had happened, together with a short poem she'd written.

God is my Rock
How high the highest rock
How low the deepest one
And all that scree
In between –

> I was halfway up or down
> When I painted it,
> But now I'm going up,
> Since being here
> And meeting with the Lord.

On the final morning of that holiday, chatting over breakfast, I and another woman realized that Anne was returning to a far-from-easy situation. The three of us prayed together, knowing that, though God had rescued Anne, just as the psalmist did, she would need a lot more help.

Months later she wrote and told me how my writing assignments had fired her up and started her thinking in a new way – yet even that was frustrating.

> I feel I may have writing talent that is being wasted, and I haven't the means or wherewithal to do anything about it. Yesterday, I wrote the following poem in about 15 minutes, it just rolled out – and then your letter arrived, asking if I would tell my story for your book.

Anne has called the poem:

> **Letting go, on the edge of holding on**
> 'I want to marry your daughter,' he said.
> 'Take care of her for ever, get wed –'
> And oh how happy a feeling it was
> To love one another for ever, because
> Life was invincible, nothing could fade
> Away the marvel of love that we made.
>
> I was the daughter, we did get wed
> But now it's my turn at caring instead.
> Years down the line and I'm feeling so sad,
> My once-healthy husband's life is so bad.
> I'm like a half-widow, I look at him there –
> No trips, no holidays, no bed to share.

It's now just a job, where once it was bliss
We still 'love' each other, but where is the kiss?
How long can I cope with emptiness there,
These feelings kept in, unable to share?
Not long, for soon I might take 'the long walk',
I feel too ashamed at my thoughts to make talk.

My tears roll down as I blink in the dark
Of my lonely long nights, and up with the lark,
But carers, they cannot afford to be ill
When life has dealt out such an oh, bitter pill!
It's time to *let go* of the life we once had,
Convert my bad thoughts, and aim to be glad.

Lord, you are our Rock. You do rescue us, time and time again – and you understand. You are more than willing to do this, we are not a 'nuisance' to you. But Lord, there are people like Anne who feel trapped – among them carers with little prospect of respite and limited resources to do anything other than the daily grind, while all their other talents 'go to waste'. Keeping a right attitude must help, but what a battle! Lord, may we be sensitive not only to pray for but to reach out and offer practical help and respite to any we know in this kind of situation, helping them to hold on until they find once again your life in all its fullness. Amen.

Endurance

Let us hold unswervingly to the hope we profess, for he who promised is faithful. And let us consider how we may spur one another on towards love and good deeds . . .

You need to persevere so that when you have done the will of God, you will receive what he has promised.

(Hebrews 10.23–24, 36)

Let us run with perseverance the race marked out for us.
(Hebrews 12.1)

Last night my prayer partner confessed that she had a real problem with healing.

> People in my church home group were so excited about spectacular healings by a Christian ministry in rich America – and I'm thinking, what about all those who died as a result of the typhoon in Burma (also known as Myanmar) or the earthquake in China?

My prayer partner has a Burmese friend and we've been praying for that country for a while, holding on to our hope in God for that and other prayers which remain unanswered.

It's not that God doesn't answer prayer. We rejoiced, looking back over notes of our monthly prayer times together, that several once-dire situations had turned right around. We thanked him too for opportunities opening up in unexpected ways – again acknowledging these as 'answers' to long-ago prayers. We commented that the way and timing in which God answers is often unspectacular – more like the miraculous but slow growth of a plant from what seems a dead seed than flash, bang – a giant tree materializing from nowhere.

Maybe the truth lies in 2 Corinthians 12.12: 'The things that mark an apostle – signs, wonders and miracles – were done among you with great perseverance.' In other words, a mature Christian will hold on – persevere – as well as letting God's signs and wonders flow through him or her when the Spirit chooses.

These are heavy matters. So here's a story which made me laugh out loud, but contains something just as profound of that same truth.

Where there's life there's hope

One of the most satisfying moments I can recall during almost 30 years of teaching in Roman Catholic primary schools was the involuntary reaction when, having ordered a dozen day-old ducklings for the children to study in class, I placed the box in which they had arrived on my desk and lifted off the lid.

There was the most beautiful, delicate, vulnerable bundle of exquisitely fluffy, wide-eyed, miniature bird life I, or the children, had ever seen. My gasp was as genuine as theirs. From that moment something gelled in the class. We were never, ever quite the same again.

We kept the ducklings in a big watertight area at the back of my large classroom. Children were begging to observe, feed, draw, write about, discuss, weigh and measure them. The whole curriculum could be taught via ducklings, I thought, until they began to produce disproportionate amounts of wet mud and very smelly droppings. Thus teachers heading for a well-earned rest and a cuppa in the staff room, children trying not to run on their way out to the playground, even people passing in the street came to know of the existence of our ducklings. The cleaners complained, so I had to allow children to take the ducklings home each evening and bring them back, fed and groomed, next morning.

Françoise arrived in the classroom one morning, tears running down her cheeks. She held a small fluffy bundle, from which hung a long fluffy neck and a duckling's head with eyes closed. The whole class 'oooed!'

'Oh dear, whatever happened, Françoise?'

'He's dead, Mr Stayne. He fell into his cornflakes this morning and drowned.'

The children, especially Françoise, were inconsolable.

I took the dead duckling in my hands. Looking carefully, I noticed a very slight movement in its gullet, as if it were feebly trying to swallow a large piece of bread. Where there's life there's hope, I thought. Thank God for clichés, sometimes they come in handy.

I gently squeezed the tiny body, trying a duckling kind of artificial respiration – nothing! Mouth to mouth? How? A milk straw inserted into the beak, a few small puffs of air into the straw . . . the little body jerked. The class 'oooed' again.

Somebody shouted, 'It's alive – Mr Stayne has brought it back to life!'

I wrapped it in a soft cloth and laid it on a radiator. Françoise was smiling from ear to ear adoringly at me. Gradually the little creature recovered, almost to normality.

Now there was talk in the playground about the possibility that I was really Jesus come again, rumours which reluctantly I felt I had to scotch. However, my standing with the children shot up – although it wasn't quite the same with the staff.

The little duckling was at a grave disadvantage from then on and was finally adopted and taken home for good by a quiet boy called Robert. Minor brain damage from its ordeal had caused inconvenient disabilities. When it tried to walk forward it found to its surprise that it went backwards – frustrating when trying to head for its breakfast cornflake dish.

But the power of love triumphed and Robert loved it from the depths of his little boy's heart. The last I heard was that it was still alive well into Robert's secondary school years.

I couldn't have given it the same love and attention – it would have driven me quackers!   (Tony Stayne)

Lord, it seems to me that, while the duckling wouldn't have lived without that brief moment of spectacular intervention, somehow it's the enduring care of quiet little Robert which brings the warmest smile to your face. Help us never to run after the spectacular for its own sake but to let the power of your love flow through us, enabling us to hold on, to persevere, especially when things don't work out as perfectly as we might have wished!

Faith

We sent Timothy, who is our brother and God's fellow-worker in spreading the gospel of Christ, to strengthen and encourage you in your faith, so that no-one would be unsettled by these trials . . . when we were with you, we kept telling you that we would be persecuted. And it turned out that way . . . I was afraid that in some way the tempter might have tempted you and our efforts might have been useless. But Timothy has just . . . brought good news about your faith and love . . . Therefore, brothers, in all our distress and persecution we were encouraged about you because of your faith . . . all the joy we have in the presence of our God because of you . . . Night and day we pray most earnestly that we may see you again and supply what is lacking in your faith. (1 Thessalonians 3.2–10)

'These three remain: faith, hope and love,' Paul says in 1 Corinthians 13.13. He means for eternity. But right now, do we hold on to faith or does it hold on to us? Even people who have a vibrant relationship with God *can* let go of their faith – I've seen it happen. Sad to say, years later they are still not walking with the Lord and one can only pray that they will find him again before they die.

This is quite different from the times most of us experience when we feel God isn't there, lose our trust in him for a while or are haunted by questions – feelings that we've been betrayed, even. Perhaps pain of body, soul or spirit so fills every sensor that he is blocked out. He's still there, though. Those are the times, as the famous 'Footprints' story says, when he carries us – though we only see that when looking back.

At other times our pain seems to draw us closer to God, as it did the Thessalonians. The Lord becomes our only hope, our best comfort. His peace and joy in those times really do pass all understanding – 'God is for real!' we say. Not only our own faith but that of others is strengthened – see how Paul, writing from prison himself, was encouraged to hear of these relatively new Christians' faith shining out under pressure!

Maybe the question's not, 'Do we hold on to faith or does it hold on to us?' but, 'Do we have faith in God or does he have faith in us?' Certainly our faith in him has to exist but not as something big, strong or unwavering – he's the huge, almighty, unchanging one and for some reason we'll never fathom, he not only believes in us but loves us!

So I guess the answer to the question lies not in faith itself but in a relationship. A child *can* run away from a loving parent, and become lost. Another child can take steps to improve her relationship with her loving father, spend more time with him and so on. But the loving parents' love for and belief in their children comes first, is stronger, understands the limitations of their little ones and, whatever happens, holds on, never giving up on them.

Eric Leat (see p. 111) is in his mid-eighties, has been a Christian for longer than he can remember and was baptized as a young man 70 years ago! Formerly an accountant, not a missionary or minister, he wouldn't say that he'd done anything spectacular with his faith. He's a neighbour of mine, living alone since his wife died after he'd seen her through nearly a quarter of a century with cancer. Not long afterwards he developed a virulent cancer himself, suffering a great deal. Yet when I say Eric's name, the face of anyone who knows him lights up. It's good to be with him. There is no need of words for his faith to shine out, encouraging us all. It's always there, quiet but strong – along with his gentle humour. One Sunday in church he read out his own 'take' on both faith and the TV programme *Antiques Roadshow* – and has given permission for me to repeat it here.

Well, thank you for bringing your faith along for us to look at. They turn up quite often and the quality and condition vary enormously. I'm sure you know that yours is not in perfect condition. But then I have yet to see one that is.

It's badly worn and broken here and there. But you say it still works quite well. Mmm, that's good. How long have you had it? Nearly 40 years! Well, in some respects the older they are the better. But really, age is not important, many of the new ones are excellent. Condition is everything.

It was a gift you say? Yes, they are always gifts, never knew one that wasn't. You know, a lot of this damage could be restored. You would need to work at it, but there's help available. You know where to go for help, of course? And I'm sure you have a copy of the handbook.

I see you've been polishing the outside. That's good, but you need to work on the inside too. Some of these hidden places could be cleaned and oiled, they don't show, of course, but it will work much better and be more reliable, more useful.

I have one too, you know. Not a very good model but it's always with me; only really look at it about once a week.

Value? Oh, impossible to say, each one is unique. No one knows how much they cost, they were paid for long, long ago.

As Eric put it, 'You know where to go for help, of course?' Because my faith stumbles from time to time, I find this verse helpful:

> The steps of a man are from the LORD,
> and he establishes him in whose way he delights;
> though he fall, he shall not be cast headlong,
> for the LORD is the stay of his hand.
>
> (Psalm 37.23–24, RSV)

We know that David's faith also stumbled and it's worth reading right through this psalm asking, 'How did David strengthen his faith in God – and how can I grow in faith and relationship with you, Lord?'

Hope

> Why, O LORD, do you stand far off? Why do you hide yourself in times of trouble?
>
> In his arrogance the wicked man hunts down the weak, who are caught in the schemes he devises . . .
>
> Arise, LORD! Lift up your hand, O God. Do not forget the helpless . . .
>
> The LORD is King for ever and ever; the nations will perish from his land.
>
> You hear, O LORD, the desire of the afflicted; you encourage them, and you listen to their cry, defending the fatherless and the oppressed, in order that man, who is of the earth, may terrify no more. (Psalm 10)

Why is it that, in times of trouble, when we feel we need him most, sometimes God seems to be a million miles away? Is he hiding? If so, he'll be extremely good at it – there will be little chance of our finding him.

What if his absence belies all that we believe about his nature? Scripture repeats so many times that he rescues the poor and needy and yet we know that doesn't always happen. It's worse when the trouble is not ours, but afflicting someone innocent and powerless, without a voice or resources of their own. Jesus called such 'the meek', pronounced them 'blessed', said they'll inherit the earth. Oh yes? It seems every time we read or hear the news we see the poor trapped, the helpless crushed – and if God forgets them, what hope is there, for any of us?

But the Bible doesn't ignore their plight. Many of the psalms cry out to God on behalf of the meek. 'How long,' they ask, 'before you act, Lord?' By the end of the psalm, although the circumstances haven't changed, often the psalmist has – somehow he's hung on to his hope in God.

Emily Bailey wrote about a little boy who touched her life when she was in Zambia with her husband and their two young children. As representatives of a small British Christian charity they were helping people in this remote region to farm more productively and to find water. Emily writes:

His name was Oliver – born into a family in the heart of the deepest Zambian bush, to a mother and father who were poor and hungry, but proud and hardworking. They had lost their firstborn son at three months old to undefined sickness. Death had just come, like an unexpected thief in the night.

Oliver was their gift.

One day when Oliver was six weeks old his mother brought him to me. 'He is not doing so well,' she said. I looked at the boy. His deep brown eyes looked back at me – or beyond me, unfocused and glazed. His head seemed swollen and the unmistakable marks of the witch doctor were upon his scalp.

'Rose, my friend,' I said gently to his mother, 'Oliver needs to see a doctor, he needs to be in hospital.'

Thus started a journey – hospital after hospital with no doctors or, at best, health workers with little skill or qualification and no medicine. At last, Oliver was taken to Lusaka and diagnosed with fluid on the brain. A shunt fitted into his head drained the fluid away. Now we had to wait – to see if Rose's precious gift would grow into the strong lively son they yearned for, or whether he would be forever tied to his mother's back, possibly blind, deaf or paralysed.

Thus, the journey continued – yet more hospitals and ill-equipped, tired personnel shrugging their shoulders and laughing in the face of the white madam standing frustrated and forlorn before them – but also a journey of discovery and faith. You see, I am a woman who still believes today in a God of unconditional love and mercy – a heavenly Father who sees and feels the pain and heartfelt cry of his children; I believe in the power of prayer. But mostly, I believed in Rose's right to see her son grow up into a strong proud African boy, and in Oliver's right to run, sing and dance for his God-given heritage.

We prayed hard, me and my African sister. I, to my God of justice, mercy and unfailing compassionate love – and she, to the God she hoped in.

We saw signs. He focused his eyes. He held his head up. The hint of a smile.

I had to leave Zambia. My own son needed to start school, and my husband's work dictated a return to the UK.

I left Rose feeling abandoned, vulnerable and afraid for her son's future, but with my assurance of God's faithfulness to her family. I truly believed my words. She had to hold on to her God of hope – and trust him with her gift.

In January 2008 I received word from Zambia. Oliver had died. The thief had returned.

I am in Surrey. I am carrying my third child, living a life of blessing, privilege and abundant gifts.

My sister, Rose, is still in rural Zambia, still poor, still hungry. No gift.

Relentless condemnation comes pounding at my door; I retreat to a dark place, confusion, anger and grief my only companions. I stay there for some time; I do not deserve to come out. I cannot face listening to my own excuses, my own justifications, my own pity.

Deeper and darker, deeper and darker.

I cannot continue. I cannot carry the burden of responsibility or the weight of guilt which crushes me daily. I must let go.

A letter comes. She is broken, but she is wearing her sorrow with dignity and unfathomable acceptance. Also, a hint of something more – hope, she is still hoping, she is still holding on to her hope.

Lord, it's often the people who are deepest in the mire of a pit who somehow find your grace, your hope. Those of us who stand there, watching, horrified, feel that, after we've done all we can, maybe we should simply give up, even on you, Lord. Nothing will bring Oliver back – but Rose has a precious gift, that of finding you, even in the deepest, darkest place. Lord, should we find ourselves in that place, may we say along with Job, 'I know that my Redeemer lives.' And meanwhile may we keep praying, hoping and helping, on behalf of the poor and meek, for indeed you love them, God.

Holding on to Love – the sound of heaven on earth

As God's chosen people, holy and dearly loved, clothe yourselves with compassion, kindness, humility, gentleness and
patience. Bear with each other and forgive whatever griev-
ances you may have against one another. Forgive as the Lord
forgave you. And over all these virtues put on love, which
binds them all together in perfect unity. Let the peace of Christ
rule in your hearts, since as members of one body you were
called to peace. And be thankful. Let the word of Christ dwell
in you richly as you teach and admonish one another with
all wisdom, and as you sing psalms, hymns and spiritual songs
with gratitude in your hearts to God.

(Colossians 3.12–16)

Using the imagery of taking off some filthy rags, Paul has
just been telling the Colossians to let go (or take off) some
bad stuff – anger, rage, malice, slander and filthy language,
lies . . . In place of all that, they are to grasp hold of and put
on all the royal robes of love listed above – that's the self-
giving, cross-facing, godly love, the greatest of Paul's three
'things that endure'.

Let's change the imagery – let's use sound. Listen in your
imagination for a moment to the ugly sounds made by all
that bad stuff. Strident, discordant, it sets our teeth on
edge. We want to fight back or hide from the aggression,
the hatred. Our ears, and hearts, hurt. Enough – we hear too
much of that noise blaring from the TV, from our streets,
even coming out of our own mouths, sometimes.

Now listen to the sounds of peace, humility, compassion,
kindness, unity, wisdom, gratitude – the sounds of him who
is Love, the sounds of heaven. They make me think of an

135

orchestra playing perfectly together, perfectly in tune, interpreting the music of the Creator with spirit and joy, moving to the rhythms of grace, enjoying spine-tingling harmonies as they interact, with melodies memorable and full of joy. Do we hear these sounds on earth? Yes, we do. It's there in the passage: 'You sing psalms, hymns and spiritual songs with gratitude in your hearts to God.' But worship is about far more than actual music and singing. Inasmuch as we allow ourselves to be 'dearly loved' by him in whose image we are made, we'll hear good sounds from our own lips and through our own actions – even though sometimes we let that slide away into our own selfish cacophony again.

Whether playing Rachmaninov or improvising around a worship song, there's an orchestra which seems to me to play the sounds of Love, the sounds of heaven – not forgetting heaven's sounds of hilarity. Fine professional musicians, all Christians, make up the Kings Chamber Orchestra – see <www.kingschamberorchestra.co.uk>. If you have the chance to attend a concert of theirs, grab it – failing that, listen to their CDs. Every person I know who has heard them is bowled over, experiencing God's presence and love, often in ways which reach exactly where each one needs Love's touch. That can happen only because the orchestra don't simply practise their music, they practise and hold on to the even more challenging sound of Love in their lives, both as individuals and when they come together.

Founder and director of the Kings Chamber Orchestra, solo cellist Gerard Le Feuvre from Jersey, writes here from his own experience of the sound of forgiveness – which features in our passage from Colossians as a key element of the love that endures.

It is my great privilege to play on a magnificent cello made around 1710 in Rome by a man who was a committed Christian. Every day I am always immensely grateful to the anonymous Jersey gentleman who paid for most of it for me. Those days have added up to 23 years now.

Cellos come in all manner of shapes and sizes, each with their particular foibles and personalities. To play well you need to work with the instrument and form a partnership, understanding its strengths and weaknesses and your own. Many spend their lives fighting their instruments to get their own way but this never produces a beautiful result. The deeper you work with the instrument, the more the sound you make reflects the very heart of you.

After playing in Toronto I had put my cello down for a moment while chatting with a fellow musician when – a most unlikely and terrible thing – a young man ran into it, kicking it into the air! With a splintering noise the instrument fell apart with all sorts of cracks, one of which you could look right through. I felt faint with shock and my stomach turned over, yet my strongest concern was to comfort the young man who had more or less collapsed in front of me, literally begging for forgiveness – as sorry as anyone ever could be.

I think people forget what an attractive quality repentance is in a person.

Overwhelmed with shock and grief, I could hardly eat for days, yet found this young man easy to forgive, as he was so earnest, and so sorry for what he had done. It occurred to me however that, to take Jesus seriously, we must learn to forgive even the embittered and unrepentant folk who hurt and damage us. We pray, 'Forgive us our sins as we forgive those who sin against us' – and maybe we do forgive our enemies, in principle. But I realized that weekend – it's possible to forgive superficially while enjoying the thought that they will be judged. My forgiveness went deeper and I felt huge burdens lifted from me as I found fresh waves of mercy for the unrepentant people with whom I had issues. The floodgates of heaven opened and a further miracle was about to unfold.

I brought my instrument back to London, to one of the greatest repairers in the world. After a good look he focused on the worst crack and said, 'That's just a historic crack; it's about time we cleaned it properly and repaired it for ever.' In another instant I saw a historic crack in my life – an incident some six years previously that had hurt me deeply in what seemed a lasting way. Time to deal with yet another issue of forgiveness!

Today, despite my deep initial shock and grief, I can't give enough thanks to the young man who accidentally damaged my cello. What a relief to be able to forgive various people in my life, even though I'd held on to unforgiveness subconsciously! But God had more. Although my cello had spun in the air and landed smash on its bridge on the stage, it didn't splinter into pieces, as it should have. The repairer thought it a miracle that it had simply opened at all the seams and that all the cracks were historic, not fresh. He gave it back to me, duly restored, clamped and glued and within two weeks I played the Dvořák concerto. My musician colleagues who know my cello well could hardly believe it. It always was one of the finest instruments around; after restoration it is even better – maybe even twice as good!

And so I can say that the sound of forgiveness is fantastic. A costly treasure of immense blessing to those who receive it and to those who give it, its beauty is unsurpassed.

Lord, help us together, as your 'orchestra' on this earth, to let go of all the discordant, unloving sounds we make which don't come from you. When we fail, when we're broken,

mend us. Help us to see that your loving expertise in re-
making means that we'll resonate with your life more than
ever before. Help us to hold on to your loving tune, played
at your time, in your rhythm and harmony. As you did with
Gerard, add your touch of miracle so that the sounds of
heaven and the sounds of Love expressed through us will
go on to fill this earth, to your glory. Amen.

Which battle to fight and which to let go?

Neco king of Egypt went up to fight at Carchemish on the
Euphrates, and Josiah marched out to meet him in battle.
But Neco sent messengers to him saying, 'What quarrel is
there between you and me, O king of Judah? It is not you I
am attacking at this time, but the house with which I am at
war. God has told me to hurry; so stop opposing God, who
is with me, or he will destroy you.'

Josiah, however, would not turn away from him, but dis-
guised himself to engage him in battle. He would not listen
to what Neco had said at God's command but went to fight
him on the plain of Megiddo. Archers shot King Josiah, and
he told his officers, 'Take me away; I am badly wounded' . . .
He died . . . and all Judah and Jerusalem mourned for him.

(2 Chronicles 35.20–24)

In my days of studying theology I struggled to remember the
bewildering number of kings of Israel and Judah mentioned
in the Old Testament. The accounts in Kings and Chronicles
usually said so-and-so ruled x years over Judah/Israel and did
evil in the sight of the Lord. Only three 'good' kings stood
out – David, Hezekiah and Josiah. Even they had their off
moments. Josiah paid for his with death.

Early in Josiah's reign he ordered repairs to the run-down
temple, bringing to light the long-forgotten 'Book of the Law'.

Josiah assembled his people, the book was read and he led them in repentance – all turning from evil to follow God again, renewing their covenant with him. Josiah cleared most pagan idolatry from the land and re-established Jewish sacrifices and worship festivals, such as Passover. As 2 Kings 23.25 says:

> Neither before nor after Josiah was there a king like him who turned to the LORD as he did – with all his heart and with all his soul and with all his strength, in accordance with all the Law of Moses.

So you could say that Josiah fought God's battles – apart from this last one which God didn't tell him to fight. He should have let the Egyptian army pass in peace. Maybe he'd become proud, feeling God was on his side rather than the other way round. He listened neither to sense nor to the Lord, merely assuming that to attack Israel's old enemy Egypt would be what God wanted of Israel's righteous king.

We may not be rulers, deciding whether or not to go to war. Nevertheless we all come across situations when it's so hard to know whether we should be fighting a battle, or letting go. How do we know exactly which battle 'belongs to the Lord'?

A former biomedical scientist, now senior lecturer in healthcare law and ethics, writes of someone who made her reassess which kind of battle she – and the health service – should be fighting.

Letting go of Emily

Weeping in a wheelchair, you sat guarded by beds of old ladies with white-plastered, traction-raised legs. A dense smell of over-boiled cabbage, disinfectant and fish wrapped its foetid breath around me. I noted your tears, your aloneness and the truncated, bandaged stump where your lower leg should have been. Not knowing what to do, I turned to my companions. 'Tell Sister,' one advised, so I hunted out the starched, dark-blue, ornate-buckled, frilly-hatted figure. 'One of the patients is crying,' I blurted out.

'That's only Emily. Ignore her.'

I walked away but Emily was still crying. Awkwardly, I went to her. 'What's the matter?'

'Why are they doing this to me?' she sobbed. I crouched alongside, hesitantly putting my arm around her. There was hardly anything to hold. 'They want to cut my leg off.

'Why can't they leave me alone? I just want to die. Why do they want to hurt me?

'What have I done? Why won't they let me go?'

Then Sister dismissed me.

You were 84, no relatives or visitors. A bedsore didn't heal, so first they amputated your foot, then below the knee. Relentless gangrene spread. The next day, under local anaesthetic because you were so frail a general one would have killed you, they amputated your leg at the hip. Three weeks later, in a stinking, silent side-room, alone, your coma slipped into death; a long, slow death by surgeons' cuts, ignored by too-busy professional strangers. They should have let you go.

Yet I never let you go. Eventually you pushed me into changing career. I dedicated my doctorate to you, Emily. I talk about you so others know your story. Then, when that moment comes, I hope they hold you in their hearts and minds, remember you as I do and are prepared to say, 'Enough, it's time to let go.'   (Dr Louise Terry)

Jesus, you know how difficult we find it sometimes to know which battle to fight. Health professionals dedicate themselves to preserving life – and that is right, but not always! You could have chosen not to die; you could have encouraged the other disciples to fight like Peter when you were arrested and made your escape. Even on the cross you could have summoned battalions of angels to rescue you. But you knew God's will – that the battle was greater than your own pain or death. When everything that had been prophesied was done, you didn't fight for life, you let go, giving up your spirit willingly to your Father.

Lord, in our difficult decision-times, help us to remember that you understand, because you went through Gethsemane. Help us, as you did and as Louise in her way is doing, where necessary to engage in a different, 'less travelled' fight, which may ultimately bring your will and your love to bear on some of earth's suffering and battle-weariness. Give us your strength to do this, your wisdom and your vision. Amen.

Conclusion – only the prisoner of Christ is free

When Sylvena Farrant took time out of her busy work with London City Mission for a visit to the USA she didn't expect to find the highlight – and the main benefit – to come from visiting a woman of 97, confined to a nursing home. Sylvena writes:

> I'd never met anyone so old before. I didn't want to visit her but American friends urged me on. Help, what would she be like – comatose? No, her face lit up as we approached and the warmth of her welcome made all my awkwardness disappear. Within minutes I felt I'd known her for years. Clearly she'd weathered many a storm but her eyes danced with life – soft with compassion, bright with the hope of what is yet to be. Her strength of character accentuated by

the weakness of her body, she took a lively interest, not in herself but in others.

The several missionaries she supported were pinpointed on a map of the world on the wall behind her. She told us that one night she woke, feeling an urgent need to pray for two of them. Months later she received a letter from the same couple, telling of a night when they were completely surrounded by violent people – who had disappeared, quite miraculously, by morning. That, of course, was the very time when she had been praying.

My friends had said that everyone who visited this frail, immobile woman came away blessed. I was no exception. That visit became a pivotal experience for me. She changed my perception of old age and fuelled my life for the future. I began working more and more with elderly people and have been privileged to meet other outstanding saints of God in their nineties. One of them spent most of her time in a hospital bed, under an oxygen mask, yet staff and visitors alike gravitated to her bedside and she was always wanting more Christian literature to give away!

Such are Sylvena's 'heroines of the faith': prisoners of their failing bodies, they couldn't be more free in the Lord – and that's inspiring. Maybe it's because they've let go of everything that isn't him.

As I've been writing this book, I've thought often of the first regular Greek verb I learnt – written phonetically it's loo-oh, to loose. Being abysmal at both classical Greek at school and New Testament Greek at university, I used to wonder why we had to learn that verb in particular. In French they taught us: 'I eat, like, take, have, am', even 'I lose' and I've chattered away in France using all of those, but never 'I loose' – what would you want that for?

Well, I've been coming to understand that to loose (or release, set free, let go) is a key God-verb. He does those things often – in Greek, Hebrew or any language. Take a look at these Scriptures, just a small sample:

> The LORD God commanded the man, 'You are free to eat from any tree in the garden.' (Genesis 2.16)

> I will bring you out from under the yoke of the Egyptians. I will free you from being slaves to them. (Exodus 6.6)

> Free me from the trap that is set for me, for you are my refuge. (Psalm 31.4)

> A light for the Gentiles, to open eyes that are blind, to free captives from prison and to release from the dungeon those who sit in darkness. (Isaiah 42.6–7)

> If the Son sets you free, you will be free indeed. (John 8.36)

> But now that you have been set free from sin and have become slaves to God, the benefit you reap leads to holiness, and the result is eternal life. (Romans 6.22)

Most important, perhaps, is Jesus' announcement at the start of his ministry:

> He has sent me to proclaim freedom for the prisoners and recovery of sight for the blind, to release the oppressed. (Luke 4.18)

He sets us free from our mess only to gather and hold, cleanse, feed, shelter and sustain us – then lets us go out in his authority to gather others.

> I will give you the keys of the kingdom of heaven; whatever you bind on earth will be bound in heaven, and whatever you loose on earth will be loosed in heaven. (Matthew 16.19)

Belonging to God, being his 'prisoner', like Sylvena's elderly heroines of faith, resolves so many of the tensions and paradoxes we've seen between our responsibilities for holding on and letting go. We can learn to trust others to one who trusts us with responsibility – then bears most of its weight on his own shoulders, if only we'll let him. Finally, although we may sometimes let go of him, he won't let go of us.

I'd like to end the book with a poem written by Alex Mowbray. As you read it, hold on . . . and let go!

Deep Love
Oh the deep, deep love of God
and what is deep?
Think oceans, waves that never sleep,
think distant shorelines full of people
wondering
what is out there . . .

Adventure meets breathtaking fear!
The call of the deep rolls in, rolls in
washing sands of disappointment, pain and
holding back.
But why so difficult to float,
to let ourselves drift out of depth?
Is not our Creator's plan
bigger than horizon's view?

Be still
remembering
that he will never let us drown.